Tucholsky Wagner Zola Scott Sydow Freud Schlegel
Turgenev Wallace Fonatne Freud
Twain Walther von der Vogelweide Fouqué Friedrich II. von Preußen
Weber Freiligrath Frey
Fechner Fichte Weiße Rose von Fallersleben Kant Ernst Frommel
Richthofen
Engels Fielding Hölderlin
Fehrs Faber Flaubert Eichendorff Tacitus Dumas
Maximilian I. von Habsburg Fock Eliasberg Zweig Ebner Eschenbach
Feuerbach Eliot Vergil
Ewald
Goethe London
Mendelssohn Balzac Shakespeare Elisabeth von Österreich Dostojewski Ganghofer
Lichtenberg Rathenau Doyle Gjellerup
Trackl Stevenson Hambruch
Mommsen Tolstoi Lenz Droste-Hülshoff
Thoma Hanrieder
Dach von Arnim Hägele Hauff Humboldt
Verne Hagen
Karrillon Reuter Rousseau Hauptmann Gautier
Garschin
Damaschke Defoe Hebbel Baudelaire
Descartes Hegel Kussmaul Herder
Wolfram von Eschenbach Schopenhauer Rilke George
Bronner Darwin Dickens Grimm Jerome Bebel
Melville Proust
Campe Horváth Aristoteles Voltaire Federer
Bismarck Vigny Barlach Heine Herodot
Gengenbach
Storm Casanova Tersteegen Grillparzer Georgy
Chamberlain Lessing Gilm
Langbein Gryphius
Brentano Lafontaine
Strachwitz Claudius Schiller Kralik Iffland Sokrates
Schilling
Katharina II. von Rußland Bellamy
Gerstäcker Raabe Gibbon Tschechow
Löns Hesse Hoffmann Gogol Wilde Vulpius
Gleim
Luther Heym Hofmannsthal Morgenstern
Roth Klee Hölty Goedicke
Heyse Klopstock Kleist
Luxemburg Puschkin Homer Mörike
Machiavelli La Roche Horaz Musil
Navarra Aurel Musset Kierkegaard Kraft Kraus
Lamprecht Kind Moltke
Nestroy Marie de France Kirchhoff Hugo
Laotse Ipsen Liebknecht
Nietzsche Nansen
Marx Ringelnatz
von Ossietzky Lassalle Gorki Klett Leibniz
May vom Stein Lawrence Irving
Petalozzi Knigge
Platon Kafka
Sachs Pückler Michelangelo Kock
Poe Liebermann Korolenko
de Sade Praetorius Mistral Zetkin

The publishing house tredition has created the series **TREDITION CLASSICS**. It contains classical literature works from over two thousand years. Most of these titles have been out of print and off the bookstore shelves for decades.

The book series is intended to preserve the cultural legacy and to promote the timeless works of classical literature. As a reader of a **TREDITION CLASSICS** book, the reader supports the mission to save many of the amazing works of world literature from oblivion.

The symbol of **TREDITION CLASSICS** is Johannes Gutenberg (1400 – 1468), the inventor of movable type printing.

With the series, tredition intends to make thousands of international literature classics available in printed format again – worldwide.

All books are available at book retailers worldwide in paperback and in hardcover. For more information please visit: www.tredition.com

tredition was established in 2006 by Sandra Latusseck and Soenke Schulz. Based in Hamburg, Germany, tredition offers publishing solutions to authors and publishing houses, combined with worldwide distribution of printed and digital book content. tredition is uniquely positioned to enable authors and publishing houses to create books on their own terms and without conventional manufacturing risks.

For more information please visit: www.tredition.com

A Peep into Toorkisthhan

Rollo Gillespie Burslem

Imprint

This book is part of the TREDITION CLASSICS series.

Author: Rollo Gillespie Burslem
Cover design: toepferschumann, Berlin (Germany)

Publisher: tredition GmbH, Hamburg (Germany)
ISBN: 978-3-8491-5008-2

www.tredition.com
www.tredition.de

Frontispiece

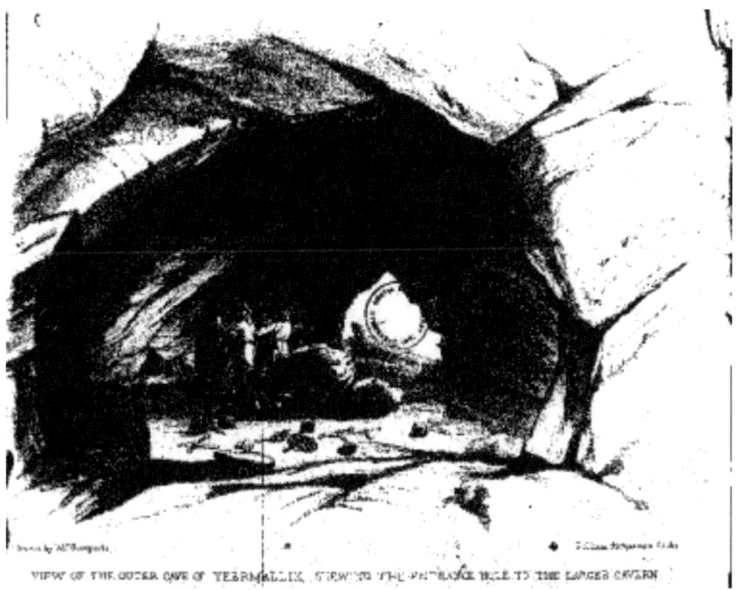

View of the Outer Cave of Yeermallik, shewing the Entrance Hole
to the larger Cavern

Drawn by Mr Gempertz
Pelham Richardson Litho

A PEEP INTO TOORKISTHAN.

BY
CAPTAIN ROLLO BURSLEM,

THIRTEENTH PRINCE ALBERT'S LIGHT INFANTRY.

1846.

TO THE RIGHT HON. THE EARL OF CARNARVON,

HIGHCLERE CASTLE.

MY LORD,

Having received your Lordship's permission to dedicate to you this my first essay as an Author, I beg to tender my best acknowledgements for the honour, and for the interest you have so kindly expressed in the success of the following pages. Under such favourable auspices a successful result may be confidently anticipated by

Your Lordship's
Obliged and obedient servant,

ROLLO BURSLEM.

HAREWOOD LODGE,
HAMPSHIRE.

TO THE READER.

The following pages are literally what they profess to be, a record of
a few weeks snatched from a soldier's life in Affghanistān, and
spent in travels through a region which few Europeans have ever
visited before. The notes from which it is compiled were written on
the desert mountains of Central Asia, with very little opportunity,
as will be easily supposed, for study or polish. Under these circumstances, it can hardly be necessary to deprecate the criticism of the
reader. Composition is not one of the acquirements usually expected of a soldier. What is looked for in his narrative is not ele-
gance, but plainness. He sees more than other people, but he studies
less, and the strangeness of his story must make up for the want of
ornament. I can hardly expect but that the reader may consider the
style of my chapters inferior to many of those which are supplied to
the public by those who are fortunate enough to enjoy good librar-
ies and plenty of leisure; two advantages which a soldier on service
seldom experiences. But this I cannot help. Such as they are, I offer
him my unadorned notes; and perhaps he will be good enough to
let one thing compensate another, and to recollect that if the style of
the book is different from what he sometimes sees, yet the scenery is
so too. If instead of a poetical composition he gets a straightforward
story, yet instead of the Rhine or the Lakes he gets a mountain chain
between Independent Tartary and China.

WALMAR BARRACKS,
   March, 1846.

CONTENTS

A PEEP INTO TOORKISTHĀN.[*]

[* Note: A portion of the following pages in their original form has appeared in the Asiatic Journal.]

———

CHAPTER I.

During the summer of 1840, the aspect of the political horizon in Affghanistān afforded but slight grounds for prognosticating the awful catastrophe which two short years after befel the British arms. Dost Mahommed had not yet given himself up, but was a fugitive, and detained by the King of Bokhara, while many of the principal Sirdars had already tendered their allegiance to Shah Sooja: and there was in truth some foundation for the boast that an Englishman might travel in safety from one end of Affghanistān to the other. An efficient force of tried soldiers occupied Ghuzni, Cabul, Candahar, Jellalabad, and the other strongholds of the country; our outposts were pushed to the north-west some fifty miles beyond Bameeān, the Khyber and Bolun passes were open, and to the superficial observer all was tranquil. The elements of strife indeed existed, but at the time when I took the ramble which these pages attempt to describe, British power was paramount, and the rumour was already rife of the speedy diminution of the force which supported it.

Notwithstanding the modern rage for exploration, but few of our countrymen have hitherto pierced the stupendous barrier of the Paropamisan range; but the works of Hanway, Forster, Moorcroft, and Trebeck, Masson, and Sir Alexander Burnes, convey most valuable information concerning the wild regions through which they travelled, and I am bound in simple honesty to confess that my little book does not aspire to rank with publications of such standard merit. An author's apology, however humble and sincere, is seldom attended to and more rarely accepted. Surely I am not wrong in assuming that a feeling of mournful interest will pervade the bosom of those who have the patience to follow my perhaps over-minute description of places whose names may be already familiar to them as connected with the career of those bold spirits who in life devoted their energies to the good of their country and the advancement of science, and who in the hour of disaster, when every hope was dead, met their fate with the unflinching gallantry of soldiers and the patient resignation of Christians.

My lamented friend, Lieutenant Sturt, of the Bengal Engineers, was one of the foremost of those who endeavoured, during the critical situation of the Cabul force previous to its annihilation, to rally the drooping spirits of the soldiers; and without wishing in any way to reflect on others, it may fairly be said that his scientific attainments and personal exertions contributed not a little to those partial successes, which to the sanguine seemed for a moment to restore the favourable aspect of our military position. But I forbear from now dwelling upon these circumstances, lest I might undesignedly give pain to those who still survive the fatal event, merely stating my humble opinion that the memory of any mistake committed, either in a political or military light, will by the noble-minded be drowned in sorrow for the sufferings and death of so many thousands of brave men.

In the month of June, 1840, Lieutenant Sturt was ordered to survey the passes of the Hindoo Koosh, and I obtained leave from my regiment, then in camp at Cabul, for the purpose of accompanying him; my object was simply to seek pleasant adventures; the "*cacoethes ambulandi*" was strong upon me, and I thirsted to visit the capital of ancient Bactria; the circumstances which prevented our reaching Balkh will hereafter be detailed, but the main object of the expedition was attained, as Sturt executed an excellent map of the passes alluded to, and satisfactorily demonstrated that almost all the defiles of this vast chain, or rather group of mountains, may be turned, and that it would require a large and active well-disciplined force to defend the principal ones. I have made every possible inquiry as to the fate of the results of Sturt's labours, but fear that they too were lost in the dreadful retreat. Whatever still exists must be in the Quarter-Master General's Department in India, far out of my reach, so that I am obliged again to request the indulgence of my reader for the want of a proper map on which he might, if he felt so inclined, trace our daily progress,[*] and to crave his forgiveness if I occasionally repeat what has been far more ably related by Moorcroft and the other authors whom I have already mentioned.

[* Note: Since receiving the proof sheets for correction I have been kindly supplied by my friend Major Wade with a map taken principally from the one executed by the late Lieutenant Sturt.]

To the traveller whose experience of mountain scenery is confined to Switzerland, the bold rocks and rich though narrow valleys of the frontiers of Toorkisthān offer all the charms of novelty; the lower ranges of hills are gloomy and shrubless, contrasting strikingly with the dazzling, yet distant splendour of the snowy mountains. It is an extraordinary fact, that throughout the whole extent of country occupied by these under features, which presents every variety of form and geological structure, there are scarcely any hills bearing trees or even shrubs; every valley, however, is intersected by its native stream, which in winter pursues its headlong course with all the impetuosity of a mountain torrent, but in the summer season glides calmly along as in our native meadows.

The multitude and variety of well-preserved fossils which are imbedded in the different strata of the Toorkisthān hills would amply reward the researches of the Geologist, and to the Numismatologist this portion of Asia proves eminently interesting, Balkh and other localities in its vicinity abounding in ancient coins, gems, and other relics of former days; and I much regret that I was unable to reach the field from whence I expected to gather so rich a harvest.

CHAPTER II.

In accordance with the golden rule of restricting our baggage to the least possible weight and compass, we allowed ourselves but one pony a piece for our necessaries, in addition to what were required for our small tent and cooking utensils, Sturt's surveying instruments being all carried by Affghān porters whom he hired at Cabul for that purpose.

On the 13th of June we commenced our ramble, intending to proceed to Balkh by the road through Bameeān, as we should then have to traverse the principal passes of the Hindoo Khosh, and our route would be that most likely to be selected by an army either advancing from Bokhārā on Cabul or moving in the opposite direction. The plundering propensities of the peasantry rendered an escort absolutely necessary, and ours consisted of thirty Affghans belonging to one of Shah Soojah's regiments, under the command of Captain Hopkins. As Government took this opportunity of sending a lac[*] of rupees for the use of the native troop of Horse-Artillery stationed at Bameeān, our military force was much increased by the treasure-guard of eighty Sipahis and some remount horses; so that altogether we considered our appearance quite imposing enough to secure us from any insult from the predatory tribes through whose haunts we proposed travelling. Our first day's march was merely to make a fair start, for we encamped two miles north-west of the city in a grove of mulberry-trees, and the wind, as usual in summer, blowing strong in the day-time, laid the produce at our feet; so that by mere-ly stretching out our hands, we picked up the fruit in abundance; for although the sun was powerful, we preferred the open air under the deep foliage to the closeness of a tent. During the early part of the night an alarm was raised throughout our small camp, and as we knew the vicinity of Cabul to be infested with the most persever-ing thieves, we naturally enough attributed the disturbance to their unwelcome visit, but it turned out to be only one of the remount horses, which having broken away from his picket was scampering furiously round our tents, knocking over the chairs, tables, and boxes which had been placed in readiness for packing outside the tent door. The neighing of the other horses, and their struggles to get loose and have a fight with their more fortunate companion, added to the braying of donkeys, barking of dogs, and groaning of the camels, gave me the notion of a menagerie in a state of insurrec-tion. The affair looked serious when the animal began to caper amongst Sturt's instruments, but luckily we secured him before any damage was done, though for some time theodolites, sextants, arti-ficial horizons, telescopes, and compasses were in imminent danger. The worst of an occurrence of this kind is, that your servants once disturbed never think of returning to rest when quiet is restored, but sit up for the remainder of the night, chatting over the event with such warmth and animation, as effectually to keep their master awake as well as each other. We started next morning at four, and marched about six miles and a half, the distances being always measured with a perambulator, the superintending of which gave Sturt considerable trouble, as it was necessary to have an eye per-petually on the men who guided it, lest they should have recourse to the usual practice of *carrying* the machine, whenever the nature of the ground made that mode of transportation more convenient than *wheeling*. This, together with taking bearings, and the other details of surveying, gave my companion plenty of occupation, not only during the march, but for the rest of the day when halted.

[*Note: lăc, lăkh (-k), n. (Anglo-Ind.). A hundred thousand (usu. *of rupees).*]

We were now encamped close to a village called Kulla Kazee, a place of no very good repute as regarding honesty; indeed, we were well aware of the predatory propensities of our neighbours; but we seemed destined to experience more annoyance from the great apprehension of being attacked which existed amongst our followers, than from any well-founded anticipation of it; their fears were not totally groundless, as it must be confessed that to a needy and disorganized population the bait of a lac of rupees was very tempting.

We had chosen a picturesque little garden for our resting place, the treasure and remount horses with the Sipahi guard being encamped about half a mile off to our rear. At about eleven at night the European sergeant in charge of the horses burst into our tent in some consternation, stating that a large band of robbers were descending from the adjacent hills to attack the treasure. Sturt immediately jumped up, and mounting his horse gallopped off to the supposed scene of action. All was quiet *without* the camp; *within* there was a terrible bustle, which Sturt at last succeeded in allaying by sending out patrols in various direction, who reported that nothing could be either heard or seen of the dreaded robbers. Being rather averse to these nocturnal diversions, especially as they promised to be of frequent occurrence, I made careful inquiries to ascertain if there were any real foundation for the alarm, but all I could learn was, that the neighbourhood had always been noted for robbers, who hasten towards the point upon the report of any party worth plundering passing near any of their forts. Possibly some robbers had gained intelligence of our treasure, and had actually appeared on the hills, but on discovering the strength of our party had retired.

The next day our route lay through delicious fields of ripening clover, in such profusion that the air was impregnated with its agreeable perfume, to a small fort called Oorghundee, remarkable chiefly for being the head-quarters of the oft-mentioned thieves, of whom I daresay the reader is as tired as we were after the mere dread they inspired had caused us to pass two sleepless nights. But we were now determined to assume a high tone, and summoning the chief of the fort, or, in other words, the biggest villain, into our presence, we declared that in the event of our losing a single article of our property or being annoyed by a night attack, we would retaliate in the morning by cutting the surrounding crops and setting fire to the fort!

The military reader, especially if conversant with some of the peculiarities of eastern discipline, will question how far we should have been justified in carrying our threats into execution. I can assure him we had no such intention; but be that as it may, our threats had the desired effect, and at length we enjoyed an uninterrupted night's rest.

On the morning of the 16th we proceeded to Koteah Shroof, the whole distance being about ten miles: but the first three brought us to the extremity of the beautiful valley through which we had been travelling ever since we left Cabul. The aspect of the country in the immediate vicinity of our path has been well described by one of the most lamented victims to Affghan ingratitude and treachery. "If the reader can imagine," writes Sir Alexander Burnes, "a plain about twenty miles in circumference, laid out with gardens and fields in pleasing irregularity, intersected by three rivulets which wind through it by a serpentine course, and dotted with innumerable little forts and villages, he will have before him one of the meadows of Cabul." To complete the picture the reader must conceive the grey barren hills, which, contrasting strongly with the fertility of the plains they encompass, are themselves overlooked by the eternal snows of the Indian Caucasus. To the English exile these valleys have another attraction, for in the hot plains of Hindoostan artificial grasses are rarely to be found, and the rich scent of luxuriant clover forcibly reminds the wanderer of the sweet-smelling fields of his native land.

But these pleasing associations were soon dispelled by the steep and rugged features of the pass through which we ascended on leaving the plain. It is called the Suffaed Kāk or White Earth, and we found by the barometer, that the gorge of the ravine was about a thousand feet above our last encamping ground. The hills on either side were ragged and abrupt, but of insignificant height: the length of the pass itself was about two miles, and from its head to Koteah Shroof the road was stony and difficult; but, as we had been careful at starting not to overload our baggage animals, they got through their work without being much distressed.

CHAPTER III.

I find it difficult to convey to the reader an adequate conception of the strange character of the hilly country we had now entered: no parts of Wales or even the varied groupings of the Swiss mountains offer a correct analogy. After passing the defile of the Suffaed Kāk the hills recede to a distance of about two miles on either side of the road, and the whole space thus offered to the labours of the peasant is very highly cultivated; but the barren rocks soon hem in the narrow valley, and as you approach nearer and nearer you find your enchanting gardens transformed into a dreary and desolate defile,-- this succession of small plots of fertile ground, alternating with short rugged passes, extends to Julrez, ten miles beyond Koteah Shroof; which latter place is an insignificant fort, situated in the centre of one of the little green spots so pleasingly varying this part of the country.

At Koteah Shroof we gained the banks of the Cabul river, a placid flowing stream, and as the neighbourhood of our camp did not offer any features of peculiar interest, I determined to try my luck in fishing; but first I had to tax my ingenuity for implements, as I had neither rod, line, nor net. A willow stick and a bit of string was all I could command; and yet my primitive apparatus was very successful, for the fish also were primitive, affording me ample sport and taking the bait with extraordinary eagerness. My occupation attracted the attention of a few peasants who gathered round me, and stood wondering what potent charm attached to the string could entice the fish from their native element. I endeavoured to explain the marvel, but was utterly unsuccessful; indeed, the peasants did not accept my explanation, which they evidently considered as a fabrication invented to deceive them and conceal my supernatural powers. The inhabitants of these valleys seemed a simple and inoffensive race, and, as in Europe, their respectful demeanour became more conspicuous as we increased our distance from the capital.

With regard to the state of cultivation of this valley––in which it resembles others generally throughout Affghanistan––wherever there is soil enough to hold the seed, the Affghān husbandman appears to make the most of it. We found here and there in profusion the pear, apple, cherry, mulberry, and luxuriant vine, and in some situations wheat, with an under-crop of clover.

On the 17th we proceeded to Julrez, a collection of wretched hovels of no interest, and on the 18th, after a march of ten miles through a succession of valleys and defiles, we reached the Kuzzilbash fort, Suffaed Kulla. About two miles before we arrived at our encamping ground we passed near the Sir-e-chusm or "fountain head," one of the sources of the Cabul river; it is a large pool stocked with a multitude of enormous fish that are held sacred by the few inhabitants of the adjoining hamlets, and which are daily fed by an aged fanatic, who for many years has devoted himself to their protection. As it would be deemed in the highest degree sacrilegious to eat any of these monsters, they are never molested, and are so tame as to come readily to the hand when offered food. Of course, my necessary compliance with the prejudices of the guardian of the fish prevented the exercise of my Waltonian propensities.

A little further on is a remarkable bourj or *watch-tower* isolated on a projecting rock, and supposed to have been built for the purpose of giving the chiefs of the little plain below, when at variance with the neighbouring mountaineers, notice of the approaching invader. At this point the valley is extremely narrow, being almost choked up with huge masses of rock hurled by the violence of some convulsion of nature from the sides of the impending precipices.

There are several minor forts in the vicinity of Suffaed Kulla, which is the largest, and is at present occupied by a Kuzzilbash chief, who took advantage a few years ago of the temporary absence of its rightful owner, and acting upon the principle of "might makes right," possessed himself forcibly of it, and has held it ever since. He treated us with great kindness and attention, sending us most acceptable presents of fruit, with food for our followers and cattle.

We here experienced to a great degree that remarkable daily variation of temperature so peculiar to these regions: in the gully the wind was bleak and cold, but when encamped under the shelter of the fort the heat from the sun's rays reflected from the smooth surface of the bare rock was so intense that the thermometer rose to 100 of Fahrenheit. While in camp at Cabul I frequently experienced the same rapid change, for it would sometimes be a hard frost at daybreak and an Indian summer heat at mid-day.

On the 19th of June we started very early, as the tremendous Oonnye pass rising to the height of 11,400 feet lay before us, and we had a full ten miles march ere we could reach our proposed halting place at the village of Uart. We soon entered the mouth of the pass, which was girt on either side by magnificent precipices; the road was narrow and slippery––of course without even an apology for a parapet––running along a natural ledge on the verge of a perpendicular cliff, and so *sheer* was the side, that from a horse's back you might sometimes have dropped a stone into the apparently bottomless ravine––bottomless, for the rays of a noon-day sun have never broken the eternal darkness of the awful chasm beneath. Had horse, camel, or man missed their footing whilst scrambling up the steep and stony pathway, nothing could have saved them from being dashed to pieces. Frequently, when rounding some projecting crag, the small treasure-box fastened on the camel literally overhung the abyss, and I held my breath and the pulsations of my heart increased as I watched horse after horse and camel after camel weather the critical point.

Before we reached Uart a poor woman of the Huzareh tribe (the most persecuted and enslaved throughout these regions) came and complained to us that her child had been seized by a band of plunderers, as she supposed, to be sold into slavery. Sturt immediately despatched a couple of the guard to recover her child if possible, and the poor woman went off with the two soldiers in the full confidence that her escort would be successful. I own that I myself was not so sanguine, but I had yet to learn how much even in these wild

mountains the British name was respected. The mother's hopes
were realized, and in the course of the day the child was recovered,
having been instantly surrendered on the requisition being made;
but I was surprised to see instead of a helpless child a fine handsome well-knit young man. The gratitude of the poor woman was
sincere; she had nothing, she said, to offer in return, but prayed that
every blessing might descend upon us and our most distant relations; that we might all become great kings; and that finally we
might be successful in conquering the country we were proceeding
to invade: vain were our endeavours to set before her in their true
light the object of our expedition.

We arrived rather late at Uart after a hard day's work, and were
not much gratified by the aspect of our camp, which was disagreeable, from its great elevation and its situation on a bleak table-land,
thinly covered with a short grass, with the strong winds of the Hindoo Khoosh sweeping across it.

Here a young woman came to our tent asking permission to avail
herself of our protection, as she was proceeding to the frontiers of
Toorkisthān to purchase slave girls for the Cabul market. She accompanied us to Bameeān, and there remained. I heard afterwards
that she did not succeed according to her anticipations, and that on
her return to Cabul she died of fever. Our English ideas of slavery
drawn from our knowledge of the varied sufferings endured by the
thousands who are annually exported from the western shores of
Africa, are opposite to those entertained in the east even by the
victims themselves. The Asiatic and African slave are alike in name
alone; the treatment of the latter in those parts of America where,
spite of the progress of civilization and the advancement of true
principles of philanthropy over the world, slavery is still tolerated
and encouraged, has been too well and too often described for me to
venture a word of my own opinion, but in Asia, in many cases, the
loss of liberty is hardly felt.

The situation of the domestic slave of Egypt (though, strictly
speaking, he must be classed under the head of "African") is analo-
gous to that observable generally in the east; and I form my opinion
partly from an anecdote related to me by my friend Captain Westmacott, of the 37th Native Infantry, who was killed in the retreat

from Cabul, which I will venture to repeat as an illustration. He was proceeding by the overland route from England to India, and remained some time in Egypt to view its splendid antiquities. On making inquiries with the object of procuring servants, he was informed that he had better purchase slaves. The civilized notions of my friend revolted at the idea, but he was assured that it was a method very generally adopted, as he would find it extremely difficult to hire servants, and if successful, they would prove the veriest rascals on the face of the earth. He reluctantly consented, and had them purchased. On his departure for India he summoned his slaves, and informed them that as they had behaved themselves well he would give them their freedom. They looked astounded and burst into tears, reminding him that instead of being kind to them he had shewn cruelty, "for where," said they, "shall we go now? Who will have anything to say to us? We shall starve and die; but if your highness will sell us again, we shall be well fed and clothed." I confess I do not see why the servants, if they really were so anxious to return to slavery, should not have sold themselves, and pocketed their own value. Throughout Afghanistān a slave is treated as an humble friend, and is generally found to be faithful and trustworthy.

CHAPTER IV.

After surmounting the Oonnye Pass, which is one of the principal defiles of the Hindoo Khoosh, we proceeded on the 20th to Gurdundewāl, a distance from Uart of about six and a half miles. The road was a gradual descent, and very rugged, leading along the bases of barren rocks, till we debouched upon the river Elbon, as it is termed by the natives, but the Helmund or Etymander of the ancients. Even here, where the stream was in its infancy, the current was so strong, that while we were fording it, one of our baggage ponies laden with a tent was carried away by its violence, and, but for the gallant exertions of our tent-pitcher, we should have had to sleep in the open air for the rest of our journey; as it fortunately happened, both animal and load were recovered; and when properly dried, neither one nor the other were a bit the worse for their washing. On the 21st we encamped near the village of Kazee, after a march of nine miles along the right bank of the Helmund, which here flows in a south-westerly direction; we could procure no supplies whatever, either for man or beast, which was the more vexatious as we had a very hard day's work in prospect for the morrow, and were anxious to recruit ourselves and cattle before attempting it. We managed well enough in spite of our compulsory fast, and on the 22d we reached Kalloo, a distance of twelve miles, after crossing the steep and difficult pass of Hadjekuk, 12,400 feet high; as we approached the summit we found ourselves amongst the snow, and experienced some little inconvenience from a difficulty of respiration; though this pass was even higher than that of Oonnye, it does not possess the same abruptness and boldness of feature which render the latter so interesting and dangerous. The hills near the gorge were so strongly impregnated with iron as sensibly to affect the needle of the theodolite.

Throughout this country, and especially amongst the Uzbegs, there is a fortified wall in the form of a square surrounding each village, with small bastions or towers at the angles. Plunder is so much the order of the day, or rather of the night, that, as a protection, the cattle and every living animal are shut up in these places at sunset; the wicket is locked and barred, and if the villagers happen to have a feud with any of their neighbours, which generally is the case, a watchman is stationed on each bastion. Truly of this land it may be said, that "what one sows another reaps," for frequently a chief forming a "chuppäo" or plundering party against his neighbour, if unsuccessful in seizing men to sell for slaves or cattle for use, reaps and carries off the corn. These chuppäos are considered among the predatory tribes very exciting affairs, as affording opportunities for the young warriors to flesh their maiden swords; but it seldom happens that these encounters are very bloody, as, in the event of one party shewing a determined front, the other generally retreats. The unfortunate Huzareh tribe are constantly the sufferers, and the traveller will recognize more slaves of that than of any other "clan."

We were now in the vicinity of the Koh-i-baba, a mountain whose granite peaks still towered six thousand feet above us, though our own camp was at least nine thousand above the level of the sea. We determined upon ascending it the following morning, but at first experienced considerable difficulty in procuring guides, not from the natives being either unqualified or unwilling to undertake the task, for they were chiefly hunters, and familiar with the paths they had themselves formed in pursuit of game, but they could not conceive why *we* should be anxious to climb the difficult height, and therefore were obstinately stupid in refusing to understand the purpose for which we required their services. At length we obtained a guide, and started next morning at half-past five: with considerable fatigue and some little risk we reached the summit after three hours walking, but the magnificent view amply rewarded us for our trouble. The peaks about us were capped with eternal snow; those below were rugged and black. The comparison of the view from the top of a lofty mountain in a hilly country with that of the sea in a storm is old perhaps, but only the truer for that very reason. It was, indeed, as if the hand of God had suddenly arrested and turned to stone varied and fantastic forms of the dark tumultuous waves.

The solemn stillness of these lofty regions was a striking contrast with the busy plains below. The mountains abound in wild sheep, which the hardy hunter pursues for days together, taking with him a slender stock of food, and wrapping his blanket about him at night, when he seeks his resting-place amongst the crevices of these barren rocks. It is seldom that he returns empty-handed if he takes up a good position over-night, for the flocks of wild sheep descend from the least accessible parts at the earliest dawn in search of pasture, and one generally falls a victim to the unerring bullet of the rested Juzzyl. The distant view of the barrier range was beautiful beyond description, for, though the peak on which we stood was the highest for many miles around us, the lofty peaks of the Indian Caucasus were many thousand feet above us. We were now beyond the range of the wild sheep, and not a living creature was to be seen save a majestic eagle, who, deeming *us* intruders where he was lord of all, sailed up along the sides of the precipitous ravines, sweeping about our heads as he soared upwards, then again wheeling downwards near and nearer, till at length I fancied him within range; but so deceptive was the distance or so defective my aim that he continued unruffled in his course, whilst the sharp crack of the rifle echoed and re-echoed from crag to crag. After satiating our gaze with these wild splendours of creation, a most unsentimental craving of the inward man warned us to descend, and we returned to Kalloo by eleven o'clock to do ample justice to our breakfasts.

We left Kalloo on the 24th, ascending by a rugged broken track to the highest point of the pass, where we came upon a fort surrounded by a small belt of cultivation divided into fields by hedgerows abounding with wild roses. I could hardly have imagined the road practicable for camels, but the cautious though unwieldy animals eventually succeeded in surmounting all difficulties, and arrived late at our encampment near a village called Topechee, the whole distance being ten miles and a half. From the crest of the pass to Topechee was a gradual descent, the road bordering a tremendous fissure, deep and gloomy, along the bottom of which a pelting torrent forced its way. The variegated strata on the mountain side, forming distinct lines of red, yellow, blue, and brown, were very remarkable, and I much regret that I had not time to devote to them most strict examination in a geological point of view.

On the 25th we started for Bameeān, passing by another Topechee a few miles further on, which is famous for its trout stream. Very few of these fish are found in the country, and only in the streams within a few miles of this spot. They are red-spotted and well-flavoured, and, as the natives do not indulge in the angler's art, they will rise at any kind of fly and gorge any bait offered. While halting a few minutes at lower Topechee we fell in with an Uzbeg warrior, a most formidable looking personage, armed, in addition to the usual weapons of his country, with a huge bell-mouthed blunderbuss at least three inches in diameter; the individual himself was peaceably enough disposed, and, contrary to the usual habit of Asiatics, made no objections to our examining the small cannon he carried. On inspecting the deadly instrument we discovered it to be loaded to the very muzzle, a mixture of pebbles, slugs, and bits of iron being crammed into the barrel over a charge of a couple of ounces of powder. On our inquiring why it was so heavily charged, the man told us with much naiveté, that it was to kill *nine* men, illustrating the method by which this wholesale destruction was to be accomplished, by planting the butt on his hip and whirling the muzzle from right to left in a horizontal direction across us all, and telling us very pleasantly that if he were to fire we should all fall from the scattering of the different ingredients contained in the blunderbuss; had we not an instant before drawn the charge from which the fellow anticipated such dire effects, we might have felt rather uncomfortable at our relative positions; but I doubt whether the owner had ever had occasion to try the efficacy of his boasted manoeuvre, as he would probably at the first discharge have been killed himself either by the recoil or the bursting of the defective and honey-combed barrel.

The approach to Bameeān was very singular; the whole face of the hills on either hand was burrowed all over with caves like a huge rabbit-warren. I am informed that these caves are the work of nature, "yet worked, as it were planned," and are occupied occasionally by travellers both in summer and winter; they are observable in many places in Toorkisthān, and, when situated high up on the face of the hill, afford a safe retreat for the hunter. The road was tolerably good for the last three miles, running along a narrow valley sprinkled with numerous forts, which are generally occupied by the Huzareh tribes, an ill-featured but athletic race.

I shall not detain the reader by any description either of the wonderful ruins of the ancient city of Goolgoolla or of the gigantic images of Bameeān, these curiosities having been ably described in Masson's very interesting work; but I was a good deal amused by the various legends with which the natives are familiar, of one of which, relating to a chalybeate spring in the neighbourhood called the "Dragon's Mouth," I shall take the liberty to offer a free version. It was related to me by an old gentleman who brought a few coins to sell, and I listened to him with some patience; but in proportion as the old fellow observed my passive attention did he increase in verbosity and pompous description. I still waited for the *point* of the story, but my friend, after exhausting his powers of speech and metaphor, was fain to wind up his tale with a most lame and impotent conclusion. I now give it to the reader, not from a wish to punish him as I was punished, but because from the prolixity of the narrator he necessarily most minutely described scenes and customs, which, though they had nothing on earth to do with the "Dragon's Mouth," may prove interesting to the reader, as illustrating the peculiarities of the people amongst whom we were now sojourning.

CHAPTER V.

"A TALE OF THE DRAGON'S MOUTH."

In the reign of Ameer Dost Mahommed Khān, when all the pomp and pride of glorious war was in its zenith at Cābul, there lived on the borders of Kulloom and Kundooz, a chieftain named Khan Shereef, whose grandfather had accompanied the illustrious Nadir Shah from Persia in his expedition through Affghanistān, and followed the fortunes of his royal master, even to the very gates of the imperial Delhi. On his return towards Persia, he had for a time intended to settle in Cābul, but "death, who assaults the walled fort of the chieftain as well as the defenceless hovel of the peasant," seized him for his own; the father also paid the debt of nature in the capital of Affghanistān, but not before the young Khan Shereef had seen the light. Growing up to manhood and wearying of the monotonous life a residence in Cābul entailed, he pursued his way across the frontier mountains of Toorkisthān, and arrived at the court of Meer Moorad Beg. Here he performed good service in the field, and becoming his master's personal friend and favourite, had a fort and a small portion of territory assigned to him. It was at the court of the Kundooz ruler that he first became acquainted with Zebah, the lovely rose of Cashmere, whom he eventually purchased from her father for his wife.[*] He started with his bride to take possession of his newly-acquired gift, an insulated fortress in the heart of a country abounding in those extensive prairies for which Toorkisthān is so justly celebrated. On these magnificent savannahs he reared the Toorkman steed, and soon boasted an unrivalled stud.

[* Note: It is customary in this country as well as in other parts of Asia to purchase the young women who may be selected for wives of their relations, the purchase money varying according to the

30

degrees of beauty.] Towards the close of the first year he became a father, an event which was hailed with extravagant joy by all his vassals, the old retainers of his father foretelling the future achievements in the foray of the young Abdoollah Reheem.

A few months had scarcely elapsed, when the anxious mother spied an old crone moving about in the court-yard; their eyes happening to meet, Zebah screamed and fell into a swoon. The young heir was instantly hurried away, but not before the old hag had cast a withering glance on the boy's beautiful face; every one was now fully convinced that he had been struck by the "evil eye," which was but too clearly proved by the event, for from that day he sickened and pined away till reduced to a mere skeleton.

Large sums of money were expended by the fond parents in the endeavour to discover a charm to counteract the effects of the "evil eye," till at length in an auspicious moment it was proposed the boy should try the efficacy of the celebrated water of the "Dragon's Mouth," which is situated at the head of the enchanting vale of Bameeān, just beyond the western limits of Toorkisthān. The slave girl who proposed this scheme related numerous and wonderful cures effected by the magic waters, and enumerated many hundred individuals, the lame, the blind, the infirm, the rheumatic, and those afflicted with *bad temper*, who had been perfectly cured by either drinking of the water or being immersed in the fountain itself. She would not be positive which mode was the best, but certain she was that the cure was perfect and permanent; she herself had been ugly and cross-tempered, and now she left her audience to judge of her character and appearance. This last proof at once determined the mother to adopt a plan, which after so many unsuccessful attempts she could not but consider as her last resource.

Khan Shereef was not quite so credulous, but what chance has a man alone against his united harem! He was so far influenced by the earnest entreaties of his disconsolate wife, that it was determined in three days he should with a strong cavalcade accompany his darling invalid to the charmed waters of Bameeān. The Toorkmān warriors were too religious to doubt the fortunate results of the experiment, and accordingly for the few days which elapsed previous to the setting forth of the expedition the fort was a scene of active preparation. Armour was burnished, swords brightened and fresh ground, juzzyls cleaned and matches got ready, so that they might produce as imposing an effect as possible, not only on the presiding spirit of the fountain, and the very questionable friends through whose territories they were about to pass, but also that they might do due honour to their lord and master.

But before proceeding with my history, I must not omit a more minute description of Khan Shereefs fort. I have already described its locality on the borders of Toorkisthān. It was situated at the base of a low conical hill, on the summit of which a look-out tower had been erected; this building was in troublesome times occupied by a party of Juzzylchees, who took their station in it, and, fixing their cumbrous pieces on the parapet, watched the approach of any hostile party, and from their commanding and protected position would be enabled to keep in check an enemy attempting to ascend the opposite side of the hill. As the nearest stream of water was full two miles from the fort, the present owner, being a man full of science and mathematical knowledge, had with unparalleled ingenuity sunk a deep and substantial well inside his walls, thus rendering his position infinitely more tenable than if his water-carriers had been daily obliged, as is the case in most places, to run the gauntlet of the enemy's fire whilst procuring the requisite supply of that indispensable article.

The fort itself was an oblong square, and required three hundred men to man its walls; it was built of mud, with a large bastion at each angle three and four stories high, and loopholed. It had but one gate, on which the nature of the defences afforded means for concentrating a heavy fire. Immediately facing the gate, and detached from buildings of inferior importance, was the Khan's own residence, and some low flat-roofed houses lining the inside of the whole extent of walls, which afforded a secure shelter to the vassals. The audience-chamber or public sitting-room was so situated that the Khān could survey the whole of the interior of his fort whilst squatting on his Persian carpet or reclining on the large soft pillow, which is an indispensable luxury for a grandee of the rank and importance of Khān Shereef.

The sides of the apartment consisted of a lattice-work of wood reaching nearly to the ceiling, and connecting the mud pillars which supported the roof; the framework was richly carved, and on slides, so as to enable the owner to increase or diminish the quantity of light and air at his pleasure.

Between the Khān's dwelling and the gate was the mosque, whose minarets towered above the walls and bastions of the fort,-- its dome was beautifully proportioned, and inlaid with agate, jasper, and carnelian, besides being wonderfully painted with representations of strange animals unknown to the common people, but which the Moollah affirmed were all taken from the life.

At this time the base of the mosque was occupied by a party of men smoking and passing the Kaleeān to each other; amongst them was one, evidently superior to the rest in age and wisdom, for his opinion was frequently appealed to by all and listened to with much deference. When not called upon to interfere he sat quiet and reserved, and to judge by his countenance was in a melancholy mood. His name was Rhejjub;--he was the oldest retainer of the family, and to him in all cases of emergency did the Khān apply for advice, which had never been given without due deliberation and almost prophetic foresight. He had only that morning been deputed to remain and guard the fort during the absence of his master, and although he knew it to be a post of honor and trust, yet he could not but consider it an effeminate duty to be left guardian of the Kochkhanah or *family*, and superintendent of the *un*chosen of the band. With him, "to hear was to obey," still he envied those who had been selected to accompany their lord. Old Rhejjub had been a great traveller in his day; had wandered over many portions of Arabia, and visited the holy city of Mecca; thus gaining the valuable privileges of a Suyud or *holy man*, which title alone was a passport and safeguard amongst even the lawless Ghilgyes and Khyberrēes of Affghanistān, it being a greater crime for a man to kill a Suyud than even his own father. Thus, whenever a Chuppao or other warlike expedition was in contemplation, Rhejjub was invariably despatched to reconnoitre and obtain information, and being a man of a shrewd turn of mind, and calculating all chances during his homeward journey, was always prepared after detailing his news to give a sound opinion as to the best plan to be pursued.

At early dawn of the proposed day of departure the whole party were summoned by the Muezzin's call to offer up prayers for their safe arrival at the "Dragon's Mouth," for the effectual cure of the young Abdoollah, and his happy return to his fond mother. Before mounting, was performed the ceremony of taking from its resting place the famous sword given to the Khān's grandfather by Nadir Shah himself. The blade was of Damascus steel, and valued alone at one hundred tomauns;[*] the ivory handle was ornamented with precious stones, and the pommel was one large emerald of great beauty and value. The scabbard was of shagreen finely embroidered in gold. This precious weapon the Suyud had the enviable office of presenting to his chief unsheathed, whilst the aged Moollah who stood by read aloud the inlaid Arabic inscription on the blade, "May this always prove as true a friend to thee as it has been to the donor." The Khān received the valued heir-loom with all due respect, and kissing the weapon sheathed and fixed it firmly to his belt.

[* Note: Tomaun, twenty rupees or about £2.]

All necessary preparations for the departure being now completed, the camel destined for the accommodation of the invalid was brought to the door of the palace, conducted by a favourite Arab who had for many years filled the office of head Surwan or *camel-driver*. The colour of the animal was almost white, and the large gold embroidered housings swept the ground; on either side was fixed a wicker-basket lined and covered with red cloth, and furnished with soft cushions; one of these held the young Khān, whilst the other was occupied by the nurse who was the original promoter of the expedition. At length the word to march was given, and the escort consisting of sixty horsemen galloped forth. Khan Shereef himself was clad in a coat of mail, and wore a circular steel head-piece, in which were three receptacles for as many heron plumes; a light matchlock, the barrel of which, inlaid with gold, was slung across his shoulder; attached to his sword-belt were the usual priming and loading powder-flasks made of buffalo's hide, with tobacco-pouch and bullet-holder of Russia leather worked with gold thread; and the equipment was completed by the Affghān boots drawn up over the loose trousers reaching to the knee, with sharp-pointed heels serving for spurs.

The procession moved on, the escort forming an advance and rear-guard, the chief galloping sometimes in front of the party, and now walking his Toorkmān steed alongside the richly caparisoned camel with its precious burthen.

Occasionally a horseman would dash out from the ranks in chace of a wild goat or sheep crossing the little frequented road, or, dismounting and giving his horse in charge of a comrade, would make a detour on foot in the hope of getting a shot at a chichore.[*] The tedious hours of march were thus wiled away till they reached the "Dundun Shikkun Kotul" or *tooth-breaking* pass, when the horsemen assumed a more steady demeanour. They were now within forty miles of the celebrated spring, which they hoped to reach on the following day.

[* Note: This is a species of partridge very abundant throughout Toorkistan.]

The Dragon's Mouth is situated four or five miles to the north-west of Bameeān, high up in the mountains in the direction of the Yookaoolung country. After a toilsome and somewhat perilous ascent the traveller finds himself at the edge of a deep ravine--or rather fissure in the rock, for the width at the top is seldom more than twelve feet--the sides presenting a ferruginous appearance, with tints varying from extremely dark to lighter shades, by reason of the soil being so strongly impregnated with ore. The low gurgling of the wonder-working stream might be heard issuing from the depths of the dark abysm.

Below, and at the only point of feasible approach for the disease-stricken, is a large cave, where the water bubbles up warm, and forming innumerable small whirlpools before it breaks again into a stream, and mingles its waters with those of a torrent below.

Here, at the base of a large fragment of rock, almost entirely covered with Arabic inscriptions and quotations from the Korān alluding to the healing powers of the well and the mercy of God, Khan Shereef and his now dismounted followers offered up prayers for success. Suddenly a huge mass of rock detaching itself from the mountain side thundered down the steep; it was hailed by all as a good omen, and the Moollah declaring that "now or never" was the auspicious moment, the child was taken from the arms of the now trembling nurse and immersed in the turbid waters. Hope elevated the breasts of the father and of the attendants, nor was that feeling fallacious, for on the following morning the invalid was pronounced decidedly better, and was again taken to the cavern, and again, with sanguine prayers and invocations, dipped into the pool.

Khan Shereef, feeling assured that he could now do no more, and trusting to the goodness of Providence, ordered a retrograde movement, and in a few days arrived at his castle with the infant nearly restored to health. A few years after the young Abdoollah was a healthy active boy, indulging in the sports of the field, and anxiously awaiting the time when he should be of sufficient age to join in the more exciting scenes of the chuppao. The old nurse, the proposer of the successful scheme, was highly honoured, and became chief attendant in the seraglio, which office she holds to this day.

"And now," concluded the old gentleman, "if my lord will choose to purchase these beautiful coins, he shall have them for whatever price his generosity may think fit to put upon them."

CHAPTER VI.

The force stationed at Bameeān consisted, at the time we were there, of a troop of native horse artillery and a regiment of Goorkahs in the service of Shah Seujah.

On our arrival, Dr. Lord, the political agent, sent us a polite note of invitation to pitch our tents near his fort, and (we) become his guests during our stay; we remained with him till the 29th, and were much gratified by his kind attention.

The quiet demeanour of the natives here was very remarkable, and as we can hardly attribute the circumstance to an inherent pacific disposition, we must the more appreciate the wonderful address displayed by the political agent in his dealings with the various parties, who in these remote mountains, as well as in more civilised countries, are ever ready to quarrel with each other, and only suspend their animosity when a common powerful enemy is to be resisted or a helpless stranger to be plundered. As it was, we reaped considerable benefit from the favourable impression made on the peasants by the authorities, for we were enabled to go out shooting, alone, and even wander unarmed amongst the hills without experiencing the slightest insult or incivility.

Indeed, at the period of which I am writing, there seemed to have been a pause in the wild passions of the Affghāns throughout the country, which was perhaps one of the fatal causes which lulled us into that dangerous feeling of security, from whence we were awoke by the most dreadful disaster that has ever befallen the British arms. Poor Dr. Lord was killed at Purwan Durrah during the short campaign in the Kohistan under Sir Robert Sale; and the other British officer, Dr. Grant, who was the medical attaché to the mission, disappeared during the retreat from Charrikār in 1841, and has never been heard of since.

On the 29th June we left Bameeān for Surruk Durrah (red valley), which is situated at the mouth of the gorge; it is a place of no importance, but the face of the impending hills has a most extraordinary appearance from the fanciful shapes of the harder rocks which jut out from the clayey sides of the mountains.

Here it was that Colonel Dennie, of the 13th, who afterwards fell at Jellālabad, with a small force of a few hundred men, completely routed the Ex-Ameer Dost Mahommed Khān, who was accompanied by all the principal Uzbeg chiefs and the famous Meer Walli of Kulloom.

A report reached the gallant Colonel in the morning, that the enemy had taken up a position at the head of the Bameeān valley; he immediately ordered a reconnoitring party to proceed in that direction, for the purpose of ascertaining whether there was any foundation for the alarm, and accompanied them himself; he was rather astonished on perceiving the enemy debouching from the hills in great force; the odds were fearfully against him in numbers, but, like a good soldier, he at once decided upon attacking without delay. He immediately opened a fire on them from his two guns, under the able superintendence of Lieut. McKenzie, and then dashing forward, drove them back with great slaughter into the narrow gorge, from whence they again attempted to advance, but were again beaten back, till at length they lost courage and broke away in every direction.

On the 30th we marched to Akrobād, a distance of ten miles. On leaving Surruk Durrah we entered the narrow gorge before alluded to; it is five miles long, and has precipitous sides, at the bottom of which rushed a foaming torrent: the formation of the hills was slate with a superstratum of limestone. On emerging from the Akrobād Pass, where there was not a breath to disturb the meagre foliage, we were suddenly surprized by a bleak piercing wind, which we were told invariably blew across the table land on which the fort is built. Although in the height of summer, the wind was intensely cold, and we were glad to take into wear the scanty supply of winter clothing which we had brought with us in case of emergency. Out of the stream running in front of the fort in less than an hour I managed to take a few well-flavoured trout, which swallowed my bait most greedily. From Surruk Durrah to Akrobād the road was, comparatively speaking, good, it being under the superintendence of Lieut. Broadfoot, who had been directed to make it practicable for artillery as far as Syghān; he had made good progress in his work, and at the period I write of, it was a very fair military road as far as Akrobād. Poor Broadfoot was slain in the gallant and desperate charge made by the officers of the 2d Bengal Cavalry at Purwān Durrah, of which I hope in the proper place to be able to give the reader a slight description.

The hills about Akrobād are so situated as to form a funnel for all the winds of the snowy range, rendering the temperature of the little table-land bitterly cold both in summer and winter--so much so in winter, that the Huzāreh inhabitants desert the fort in autumn for some more sheltered locality, and return again with the spring.

We now entered Toorkisthān, the pass of Akrobād dividing it from Affghanistān. Should the traveller form his opinion of the country beyond by the specimen now before us, he would be loth indeed to proceed, for a more dismal corner can hardly be conceived. The outline of the adjacent mountains was dreary and uninviting, with very little cultivation in the valley, which also bore a most desolate aspect--it was barren and unpromising, without participating in the wild and grand features which generally characterize these regions. Fuel was with difficulty procured, and our camp was but scantily furnished with even the most necessary supplies.

CHAPTER VII.

On the 1st of July we left this sad region, and pitched our tents some five miles further onwards, in a pleasant meadow, where we met a brother of Dost Mahommed, the well-known Sirdār Jubber Khān, who arrived in the course of the day from the interior of Toorkistān, and encamped close to us. He was then on his way to Cabul, having in charge the women and children belonging to the seraglio of the ex-king. He invited us to pay him a visit, which we did in uniform, and found him an agreeable old gentleman, with manners far more polished than the generality of his countrymen, who, though not deficient in a certain national savage grace, frequently shock our European notions of propriety by their open disregard of what we are accustomed to consider the decencies of society; but Jubber Khān seemed to have all the good qualities and few of the vices so prevalent in the Affghān character. No doubt that superior polish of manner was derived from his more extensive intercourse with Europeans. During our visit he presented us each with a small silver Mahommedan coin, saying at the same time with peculiar grace and dignity that he was now a poor man, and entirely dependent on the generosity of the British; that the coin was of no intrinsic value, but still he hoped we would remember the donor. Much as we respected the character of our host, I could not but regret that he had not yet picked up the English habit of sitting on a chair; for what with tight pantaloons and a stiff uniform, I got so numbed by sitting cross-legged like a tailor, that when the interview was over I could not rise from my cramped position without assistance, much to the amusement of Jubber Khān, whose oriental gravity was entirely upset.

I was informed that on being requested by the British authorities
to deliver up the family of his brother, he boldly refused, stating
that they were given into his charge, and that he deemed it a sacred
trust not to be betrayed by any consideration of personal advantage.
It will be gratifying to the reader to know that this manly refusal
did not operate to his prejudice in the opinions of those to whom it
was made. He subsequently obtained from the Dost permission to
comply with the demand, and was now on his journey for that purpose; but though he professed to have every confidence in our honour and generous kindness with regard to the females, he appeared
somewhat anxious as to the influence which his previous refusal
might have with reference to his own treatment. Jubber Khān's
name was in great repute amongst the Affghāns, who, all wild and
savage as they are, still have sufficient feeling to admire in others
those virtues which are so rarely met with amongst themselves: he
is considered an able politician also, as well as the poor man's
friend--high and low find him equally easy of access, and he is the
general mediator in quarrels between the different chiefs, and the
principal counsellor in the national debates.

Whilst encamped here the united seraglios of Dost Mahommed
and Jubber Khān passed in front of our tents, on their way to Kābul.
It was a very large procession, consisting of nearly eighty camel
loads of fair ones of every age and quality. Each camel was furnished on either side with a large pannier, and in each pannier was
a lady--weight against weight. The presence of Englishmen so
much excited their curiosity that we were enabled to enjoy a nearer
and better view of the beauties than strict decorum would have
justified, and it may not perhaps be uninteresting to my fair readers,
if, turning to advantage this slight impropriety, I here take the liberty of describing as much as I could observe of the very remarkable
travelling costume of the female Affghān aristocracy. When in public the highborn Affghān lady is so completely enveloped by her
large veil (literally sheet), that the person is entirely concealed from
head to foot; there are two eyelet holes in that part of the sheet
which covers the face, admitting air and light, and affording to the
fair one, herself unseen, a tolerable view of external objects. I trust I
may be permitted without indiscretion to remove this shroud and
give some slight description of the costume.

Over a short white under-garment, whose name of Kammese[*] sufficiently denotes its use, is a Peirān or jacket, which amongst the higher classes is made of Bokhāra cloth, or not unfrequently of Russian broad cloth, brought overland through Bokhāra. This garment is generally of some glaring gaudy colour, red or bright yellow, richly embroidered either in silk or gold; it is very like the Turkish jacket, but the inner side of the sleeve is open, and merely confined at the wrist with hooks and eyes. A pair of loose trousers, gathered at the waist with a running silken cord, and large at the ankle, forms a prominent feature in the costume, and is made either of calico, shawl-cloth, or Cachmere brocade, according to the finances of the wearer. Instead of stockings they wear a kind of awkward-looking linen bag, yellow or red, soled with thick cloth or felt, the top being edged with shawl-cloth. The shoes are similar to the Turkish slipper, with the usual Affghān high-pointed heels tipped with iron; and as these articles must from their shape be an impediment to walking, I presume that the real use to which they are generally put must have given rise to the common expression in Hindoostān for any punishment inflicted, the term being "jutte mar," literally, beating with the shoe. The weapon put to this purpose would be very formidable, and I have little doubt that the beauties of the harem keep their lords in high discipline by merely threatening with such an instrument.

[* Note: Anglice, Chemise. It may fairly be inferred that the name of this under-garment is derived from the word mentioned in the text; and doubtless there are many words in our own as well as in other modern languages that may equally be traced to Asia; for instance, Sheittan, Satan.]

On the head of the Affghān female is worn a small skull cap, keeping in place the hair in front, which is parted, laid flat, and stiffened with gum, while the rest hangs in long plaits down the back.

Next day we left for Syghān, and after a march of about fifteen miles pitched our tents in the vicinity of the principal fort. The whole journey was through a deep defile, except about half-way, when we came upon a small but well cultivated plain, with a fort in the centre. The contrast was pleasing after travelling so many miles amidst the dark overhanging crags, threatening destruction on the passer-by; but this relief was of short duration, for after two miles it gradually contracted, and formed a continuation of the defile down to the valley of Syghān.

The fort is on a small hill detached from the main range, but easily commanded, though it is said for ages to have been deemed impregnable, till some chief more knowing than his neighbours hit upon the very obvious expedient of lining the overhanging range with Juzzylchees, and picking off every individual who ventured to appear on the battlements. It is now in our possession, and occupied by two companies of Sepoys; and though the place might be seriously annoyed by musketry from the adjacent hills, still the sides of those hills are so rocky and precipitous that cannon could not be brought to bear from the summit without immense labour.

These hills are composed of sandstone and indurated clay, in which numerous fossils abound.

The valley along which we proceeded produces many varieties of fruit, and is rich in the cultivation of artificial grasses, lucerne being the most abundant.

On arriving at our encamping ground on the 3rd of July, about four miles and a half beyond Syghān, a poor villager, a vassal of Mahommed Ali Beg's, to whom the fort of Syghān belonged previous to its cession to the British, came to complain that some of our baggage animals had injured one of his fields by trampling down his grain. Upon enquiry his story was found to be correct. Mahommed Ali Beg happened to be paying us a visit when the man presented himself, and wished to drive the poor fellow away to prevent his troubling us; and great indeed was the wonder and astonishment shewn by all the natives about us when Sturt desired that the peasant should receive ten rupees as compensation for the damage done to his crops.

Loud were the praises bestowed upon our *extraordinary* justice; and Mahommed Ali Beg, forgetting the line of conduct he had but a moment before advocated, delivered the following expression of his reformed opinion in a loud pompous tone, whilst his followers listened, open-mouthed, to the eloquence of their now scrupulous chief: "Although the Feringhis have invaded our country they never commit any act of injustice;" then, having delivered himself of this inconsistent speech, he lifted a straw from the ground, and turning round to his audience, continued: "they don't rob us even of the value of *that*; they pay for every thing, even for the damage done by their followers." Corporal Trim's hat falling to the ground was nothing to the effect produced by the comparison of the straw; but, alas for human nature! I had but too strong grounds for suspecting that, of the ten rupees awarded to the peasant, seven were claimed by Ali for having induced the Feringhis to listen to the claim!!

The surrounding hills have here as at Surruk Durrah the appearance of ruined castles, with donjon or keep and tower; they forcibly reminded me of the "Castle of St. John," in Scott's Bridal of Triermain, but my visions of Merlin and fair maidens awoken from their charmed slumbers were destroyed by the sight of a little purling brook which promised me a few hours angling. Nor was I disappointed; for in a short time I (being unprovided with my fishing basket) filled two towels full of fish, and congratulated myself on my sport; however, to use an old phrase, "the proof of the pudding is in the eating," and so we found it, for when brought to table "my catch" fell far short of our epicurean anticipations, and I almost regretted that I had not continued my dreams instead of disturbing the finny tribe.

A complaint was made to us in the course of the day, that an Huzareh female, returning to her own country with one attendant, had been seized and carried away to one of the adjacent forts, where she was detained; and our interference was requested with a view to obtaining her release. We were of course most anxious to help the poor woman, especially as it appeared from what was reported to us that there were not the slightest grounds for the outrage, beyond the helplessness of her situation and the natural cupidity of the robber chief of the fort; but, unfortunately, we were travelling without credentials, the Envoy having declined to furnish us, lest the inhabitants should fancy that we were vested with any political power; and therefore we could not interfere, and what became of her I know not, though we were afterwards told that on her resigning her trinkets as her ransom she would be released. Indeed the personal ornaments of the petty chiefs are generally the point of some lawless proceeding like the one alluded to, as they are seldom possessed of sufficient capital in specie to purchase jewels, but exchange their grain and fruits for clothes and precious stones. I have mentioned the above circumstance to give the reader some notion of the lawless state of society, deeming it out of keeping with the humble character of this simple narrative, and perhaps beyond the ability of the writer, to enter more minutely into the various causes which have contributed to bring the country into so unhappy a state.

CHAPTER VIII.

On the 4th July our route lay across the Dundun Shikkun. Kotul, or "tooth-breaking pass," and a truly formidable one it is for beasts of burden, especially the declivity on the northern side. Very few venture upon the descent without dismounting, for the surface of the rock is so smooth and slippery, that the animals can with difficulty keep their legs even when led, and many teeth, both of man and horse, have been broken before reaching the bottom.

The valley of Kāmmurd lying at the foot of the northern side of the pass has a very fertile appearance, and orchards of different descriptions of fruit-trees are interspersed throughout the cultivation. The fort of the principal chief, named Uzzuttoollah Beg, from whom we received a visit, is high up the valley, and there are two others of minor importance on either bank of the river, lower down and together.

Uzzuttoollah Beg was in appearance a very fine old man with an imposing white beard; he was six feet high, large boned and muscular, and by far the most powerful and stately looking personage we had hitherto met; but he was a shrewd wicked old fellow, and when the star of British prosperity began to wane, proved himself a dangerous enemy. His own vassals, from whom he exacted the strictest obedience, stood in great awe of him. He came merely, he said, to pay his respects, to chat over political affairs, and to inquire from us whether the English intended giving up his valley to the Meer Walli of Koollum. We could give him no information as to the intentions of Government. "Khoob (well,)" answered he, "if such really be the case, the Meer Walli may seize me if he is able, provided *you* keep aloof; the Meer has tried that game before now, but did not succeed; on two separate occasions he has visited my fort in an unceremonious manner, and with hostile intent; but, gentlemen, there are two sides to a fort, the inside and the out. I was in––the Meer was out, and I kept him there; till, (suffering no other inconvenience myself than the deprivation from riding for a few days,) by keeping up a constant fire on his ragamuffins, I one fine day compelled him to beat his retreat:" and so saying, he stroked his beard with much complacency, evidently considering it and its owner the two greatest wonders of the Toorkisthān world.

It may be as well to remark here, that in these valleys as throughout Affghanistān in general, the forts are made of mud, the walls being of great strength and thickness; they are built gradually, and it takes many months to erect a wall twenty feet high, as each layer of mud is allowed to bake and harden in the sun before the next is superimposed. Now, as none of the chiefs possess cannon, except the Meer Walli and Moorad Beg of Koondooz, it is almost impossible to gain an entry into a well-constructed fort, except by treachery; and even the few honey-combed pieces of small calibre possessed by the above chieftains would not have much effect against the massive ramparts.

But the Uzbegs have a method of undermining the bastion, by turning the course of some convenient stream right under the very base; this gradually softens the lower stratum of mud, and diminishing its tenacity, the whole fabric comes tumbling down from its own weight. They also have frequently recourse to mining, but for either method to succeed the defenders cannot be on the alert.

A man who had been engaged in an operation of the latter kind, by which the fort of Badjghār was once taken, explained to me the plan adopted, which bears a rude analogy to the modern plan of mining under the glacis to the foot of the counterscarp.

To-day a horseman came into our camp at about 3 P.M. with letters from Bameeān; he had left early in the morning, and thus accomplished a journey of fifty miles with the same horse, over two severe passes, and through a succession of difficult defiles. On alighting, he tied his horse to the branch of a tree, merely loosening the girths, but not intending to give him food till the evening. The horses are habituated to the want of any midday feeding, and at night and morning seldom get grain. But the dried lucerne and other artificial grasses with which they are supplied must afford them sufficient nourishment, as they are generally in very good working condition; they are undersized, but very sure-footed; it is indeed astonishing over what fearful ground they will carry their riders. The yabboo is a different style of animal, heavier built and slower; its pace is an amble, by means of which it will get over an immense distance, but it is not so sure-footed.

I remarked that aged horses were very rarely met with, and on inquiring the reason, was informed that the horses were all so violently worked when young as soon to break down, after which they are slaughtered and made into *kabobs*. I was assured that the eating-shops of Cabul and Kandahār always require a great supply of horseflesh, which is much liked by the natives, and when well seasoned with spices is not to be distinguished from other animal food.

At this station fruit was in great profusion; I observed that the sides of a barren hill near our camp were of a bright yellow tint for upwards of a mile and a half, and on approaching to discover the cause, I found the whole space covered with apricots placed side by side to dry in the sun. I tasted some of them, which had apparently only just been gathered, and found them very well flavoured, though generally speaking I must allow that the fruits of these valleys are inferior to those of Europe, with the exception of the grape, which is unequalled. But the grape and apricot are not the only fruits which flourish in this green spot surrounded by barren rocks,--the walnut, the peach, mulberry, apple, and cherry, also come to perfection in their respective seasons.

At sunset Uzzuttoollah Beg sent us a plentiful supply of fruit, grain for our cattle, and flour for the servants, regretting at the same time that he was not able to send us sheep enough for the whole party. When he came to take leave, we told him we had received more than we expected or required, and begged his acceptance of a loonghee or *headdress* in remembrance of us. He was much gratified with the trifle, it being of Peshawurree muslin, a kind much sought after and prized by the Uzbegs. He immediately took off his own turban, which was indeed rather the worse for wear, and binding the new one round his head, declared with a self-satisfied look, that "it would be exceedingly becoming." He then arose, and probably to shew his knowledge of European breeding, gave me such a manly shake of the hand as made me expect to see the blood start from the tips of my fingers. I am not sure, with all due respect for the good old custom of shaking hands, that I should not have preferred submitting to the Uzbeg mode of salutation. On approaching an equal, the arms of both are thrown transversely across the shoulders and body, like the preparatory attitude of wrestlers in some parts of England, then, placing breast to breast, the usual form of "salaam aleikoom" is given in a slow measured tone. But on horseback the inferior dismounts, and, according to the degree of rank, touches or embraces the stirrup.

The valley of Kammurd is of an oblong form flanked by stupendous mountains; the enormous barrier of the Dundun Shikkun almost precludes the possibility of bringing cannon from the south, although one gun is known to have been dragged over by sheer manual labour; it was brought by Dost Mahommed from Cabul to quell some refractory chiefs, the carriage being taken to pieces, and the gun fastened by ropes in the hollowed trunk of a tree.

On the 5th of July we reached Piedbāgh, five miles further down the valley, which gradually decreased in breadth, seldom exceeding two hundred yards, and sometimes contracting to fifty. Along the banks of a muddy river flowing through the centre of the narrow vale, the sycamore tree was very luxuriant, and two or three forts formed a chain of communication from one end of the cultivated land to the other. Piedbāgh, as its name implies, is a complete orchard, *piedan* meaning perpetual, and bāgh, garden; from a distance it looks like a thick wood with the turrets of the forts overtopping the dark foliage. We took advantage of the quiet beauty of this spot to give our horses a day's rest, and lucky it was for us we had at Bameeān exchanged for stout yaboos the unwieldy camels which we had brought from Cabul; the yaboos get over the ground twice as fast as the camel, and for mountainous districts are infinitely preferable to the "ship of the desert."

It was lucky also that we had not burdened ourselves with bed-steads or charpoys, as they are called in the East (literally *"four feet"*); they would have inconvenienced us much; and we should, probably, have been forced to abandon them on the road, the pathways along the glens being often so narrow, and so encumbered with the detritus from the overhanging mountains, as to make it necessary to pack our baggage very compactly; inattention to this important point in mountain travelling is sometimes followed by very serious consequences, for the chair or bedstead, projecting far beyond the centre of gravity of the unfortunate animal, catches against a corner of rock, and both load and pony run imminent risk of being hurled into the abyss below. We were now so inured to sleeping on the ground, that had it not been for the multitudes of fleas we should never have felt the want of a more elevated sleeping place. The animal and vegetable character of Piedbāgh may be stated in a few words--apricots and fleas are in abundance, the former very large sized, and the latter healthy.

In the course of my journal I hope to be able to relate the circum-stances of a very pretty little affair which occurred here, some months after we passed through, between two companies of Shah Soojah's Goorkah regiment and the inhabitants of the neighbouring forts. The Goorkahs, upholding their well-known character, fought desperately against an overwhelming force; they would have suf-fered severely but for the able conduct of their leader, who was an European non-commissioned officer and quarter-master sergeant of the corps; his manoeuvring would have done credit to many an older soldier.

On the 7th July we quitted Piedbāgh for Badjghār, the most west-erly of our advanced posts; it was occupied at the period of which I write by Captain Hay, and was the head-quarters of the Goorkah battalion. The hills from a little above Piedbāgh encroach so much upon the valley as to reduce it to little more than a ravine forming two gigantic walls, that on the right being inaccessible save to the wild goat, whilst the left-hand boundary, though still precipitous, may be surmounted by active light-armed troops. On emerging from the orchards we came upon a grass meadow extending to the fort of Badjghār, which is again situate at the mouth of a defile lead-ing to Māther, the route we eventually pursued. The fort is capable of containing about two hundred men; when first taken possession of it was literally choked with filth and abominations of all kinds, but the industry of the little garrison had succeeded in giving it an air of cleanliness and comfort. As a military position it is most faulty, and it is really astonishing to conceive how heedless those who fixed upon it as a post of such importance must have been of the manifold weakness of the place; from the surrounding heights it has the appearance of being situated in a deep dyke; it is completely hemmed in, and juzzaelmen occupying the adjacent hills could easily find cover from whence they might pour in so destructive a fire as to render the place untenable. In addition to these defects, the fort of Badjghār is unprovided with a well within its defences; this, as has before been remarked, is a common case, but still it would materially affect the integrity of a force within, as they would be reduced to the necessity of frequent sallies to the neighbouring stream to obtain water.

We found Capt. Hay in no enviable position; he had but one European to assist him in his various important duties; the three or four officers who were nominally attached to the corps being either on detachment or other military employ, so that with such slender aid as one European sergeant, it was very hard work for him to keep up discipline amongst a brave but half savage band, to provide for their subsistence, keep a sharp look-out on his front and flanks, and remain on good terms with the neighbouring chiefs, whose conflicting interests, lawless propensities, and savage nature were continually requiring his mediation or interference.

"Quem deus vult perdere prius dementat" is an old saw most applicable to the conduct, or rather want of conduct of the "powers that were" during the spring of 1841, and the state of the important outpost of Badjghār is a type of the condition of most of the detached posts throughout the kingdom of Cabul; the dreadful catastrophe which ushered in the year 1842 is but too unanswerable a proof of the opinion I here express; and though innumerable instances of individual gallantry as well amongst the unlettered privates as the superior officers have thrown a halo round their bloody graves, the stern truth still forces itself upon us, that the temporary eclipse of British glory was not the consequences of events beyond the power of human wisdom to foresee or ward off, but the natural results of

an overweening confidence in our power, and of an infatuated blindness to the sure indications of the coming storm which for many months before it burst darkened our political horizon.

It will easily be believed that the various duties entailed upon Capt. Hay left him but little time for scientific researches, yet this indefatigable officer had already made a fine collection of geological specimens from the adjacent hills. I regret that circumstances prevent me from giving any of the useful information which his industry supplied. I am only able to say, that the fossils were generally found in tertiary deposits, and were plentiful in quantity, but the variety was not great. He had at the time of our visit made, likewise, considerable progress in putting his position into as good a state of defence as circumstances allowed; of course he had not means to defilade his fort, but he had erected a breastwork four feet and a half high across the defile, which would certainly be of great use in checking any body of horsemen who might advance from the north, at least for a time sufficient to enable the garrison to prepare for an attack. The fort seemed a focus for all the rays of the sun, and was intensely hot, the thermometer ranging from 95 to 110 in the shade; nor was the situation healthy, for a great many Goorkahs were in hospital, and all were more or less debilitated from the effects of the climate.

Whilst at Badjghār we made the acquaintance of one of the chiefs, Suyed Mahommed of the Dushti Suffaëd or *white desert*, through whose country we eventually travelled; we found him an easy good-tempered man, well inclined towards the British, but grasping and avaricious. Throughout our intercourse with him he behaved well, but he took occasion frequently to remind us we were not to forget that he looked for a reward; still, in summing his character, I must say he was superior to his "order;" for, either from the wish to lead a quiet life or from his limited means and unwarlike disposition, he was not given to feuds or chuppaos like his neighbours. He sent rather a characteristic letter to Shah Pursund Khān, a chief whose dominions were also on our line of route, recommending us to his notice, but concluding by telling him to judge of us and act according to our merits.

CHAPTER IX.

On the 9th July we bade our kind friend Capt. Hay farewell, and many were the prayers offered up for our safe return; the Goorkah soldiers even accompanied us for three or four miles. Sturt had not been supplied with any introductory letters from Sir William M'Naghten, although he was sent on duty, for it was uncertain what kind of a reception we might meet with amongst the chiefs of Toorkisthān, and it was therefore deemed unadvisable to give us the character of accredited agents, which would necessarily tend to mix us up with politics. Though this plan may have been very wise on the part of Government, yet it by no means contributed to our comfort, as we found ourselves frequently the objects of suspicion. Some of the chiefs plainly said, "you are come to survey our country, and eventually to take possession;" but most of them cared very little whether we came as friends or foes: they had little to lose and everything to gain by a *row*. With a few of the more influential chiefs the case was different; if we had caused Dost Mahommed, the all powerful Ameer of Cābul, to become a fugitive, what chance had they if our views led us across the Hindoo Khoosh? Such was their mode of reasoning; but it must be confessed that they were ignorant of the immense advantage the rugged nature of their barren land would give them over a regular army, and thus they were unable to form an idea of the value of the resistance which a few determined mountaineers might oppose. Amongst other wild schemes, I fancy that the idea was once entertained, or at all events the question was mooted, of sending a force to Bokhārā to procure the release of poor Stoddart. Without dwelling upon the enormous sacrifice of life and treasure which such an expedition of magnitude sufficient to ensure success would entail, I may be permitted to point out what from personal observation I have been led to consider as the "least impossible" route. The line I should recommend would be the one we pursued as far as Koollum, when the force should so shape its route as to avoid the great sandy desert, which extends for three hundred and fifty miles from Koollum to Bokhārā, by keeping to the north,

and "striking" the Oxus, which is navigable for boats of heavy burthen for many hundred miles above the capital. But even on this
plan we must suppose the force to have already surmounted the
thousand and one passes which occur between Cabul and Koollum.
Much has been printed and a great deal more written and wisely
left *un*printed concerning the practicability of these routes for a
modern army; it savours of a useless truism to state, that if the government making the attempt has resources sufficient in men,
transport, and treasure, and dwells not upon the sacrifice of these
three necessaries for an army, the thing may be done; but I can
hardly conceive any crisis in political affairs which could render
such a measure advantageous to the party undertaking it. The advancing force will always suffer, whether it be Russia advancing
upon India, or India advancing towards Europe. The hand of God
has fixed the tremendous barrier; woe to him who would despise
the warning.

Our route lay along the usual green vale so often described,
bounded by barren hills, over which a few inhabitants might occasionally be seen stalking along in their dark-coloured garments,
which harmonized with the sombre character of the country. We
pitched our tents near the little fort of Māther, about five miles from
our last encampment, and situate at the foot of the Kara Kotul, or
black pass. Our resting place afforded nothing remarkable; and indeed I feel that some apology is due to my readers for the unavoid-
able sameness of the details of this part of our journey; but I am in
hopes that this very defect, though it render the perusal of my journal still heavier, will assist in conveying an accurate idea of the nature of the country; it is not my fault if we met with no adventures,
no hairbreadth escapes, or perilous encounters. I must once more
crave indulgence.

The Affghān soldiers of our escort did not much relish the discipline I enforced. A complaint was made to me in the course of the
day by a peasant, that these warriors had most unceremoniously
broken down hedges, and entering his apricot orchard, had commenced appropriating the fruit, responding to his remonstrances
with threats and oaths. I thought this a fine opportunity to read my
savages a lecture on the advantages of discipline and regular pay. I
asked them whether they were not now much better off than when

employed by their own countrymen, and whether they expected to be treated as regular soldiers, and still be allowed to plunder the inoffensive inhabitants? One of the men, who was evidently an orator, listened to me with more attention than the rest, but with a look of evident impatience for the conclusion of my harangue, that he too might show how well he could reason. "My lord," said the man, putting himself into an attitude worthy of the Conciliation-Hall, to say nothing of St. Stephen's, "my lord, on the whole your speech is very excellent: your pay is good––the best, no doubt, and very regular; we have not hitherto been accustomed to such treatment; though you brought the evil the remedy has come with it; your arrival in Cābul has so raised the price of provisions that we could not live on Affghān pay; we have, therefore, entered the service of the foreigner; but had we received the same wages we now get from you, we should in our own service have been gentlemen." Here the orator made a pause, but soon imagining from my silence that his speech was unobjectionable, he boldly continued; "but there is one powerful argument in favour of the Ameer's service, *he* always allowed us on the line of march to plunder from every one; we have been brought up in this *principle(!!)* since we were children, and we find it very difficult to refrain from what has so long been an established practice amongst us: we are soldiers, sir, and it is not much each man takes; but the British are so strict, that they will protect a villager or even a stranger:" this last sentence was evidently pronounced under a deep sense of unmerited oppression. "But," continued he, "look at that apricot orchard on the right, how ripe and tempting is the fruit; if we were not under your orders, those trees would in a moment be as bare as the palm of my hand." But I remarked, "would not the owners turn out and have a fight; is it not better to go through a strange country peaceably and making friends?" "*They* fight," answered my hero; "oh! they are Uzbegs and no men, more like women––one Affghan can beat three Uzbegs." I was not quite satisfied how far the vaunted pay and discipline would prevail over the natural lawless propensities of *my army*, and in order not to try their insubordination too much, I conceived that a compromise would be the wisest plan, and giving them a few rupees, I desired them to make the most they could out of them. Off they went highly delighted with the results of the interview, clapping their orator on the back, crying out *shābash, shābash, bravo, bra-*

vo, and evidently believing the gift of the rupees as entirely due to the eloquence of their comrade. They are a simple people with all their savage characteristics, but it is very sad to contemplate a whole nation as a race of systematic plunderers.

In the afternoon the chief of Māther called to pay his respects, bringing a present of fruit and sheep's milk; the latter I found so palatable, that I constantly drank it afterwards; it is considered very nutritious, and is a common beverage in Toorkisthān, where the sheep are milked regularly three times a day. Goats are very scarce, cows not to be seen, but the sheep's milk affords nourishment in various forms, of which the most common is a kind of sour cheese, being little better than curdled milk and salt. Tea is also a favourite drink, but is taken without sugar or milk; the former is too expensive for the poorer classes, and all prefer it without the latter. Sometimes a mixture such as would create dismay at an English tea-table is handed round, consisting principally of tea-leaves, salt, and fat, like very weak and very greasy soup, and to an European palate most nauseous. We could never reconcile our ideas to its being a delicacy. Tea is to be procured in all large towns hereabouts, of all qualities and at every price; at Cābul the highest price for tea is £5 sterling for a couple of pounds' weight; but this is of very rare quality, and the leaf so fine and fragrant that a mere pinch suffices a moderate party.

What would our tea-drinking old ladies say for a few pounds of that delicious treasure? This superfine leaf reaches Cabul from China through Thibet, always maintaining its price; but it is almost impossible to procure it unadulterated, as it is generally mixed by the merchants with the lesser priced kind. The most acceptable present which a traveller could offer in Toorkisthān would be *fire-arms* or *tea*; the latter is a luxury they indulge in to excess, taking it after every meal; but they seldom are enabled to procure it without the lawless assistance of the former.

On leaving Māther we commenced the ascent of the Kara Kotul or Black Pass, which lasted for seven long miles and was very fatiguing. The large masses of rock on either side the pathway were of a deep brown colour. From the length and steepness of the ascent, this pass must be higher than any we had hitherto surmounted; the descent on the other side is difficult in proportion. The approach to Doaūb is through one of the most romantic glens conceivable. It is here that the Koollum river takes its rise; it flows due north and soon reaches a mountain meadow, where it unites with another stream coming from the east, whence the name of the Doaūb (two waters) is given to this district. In this defile are scattered huge rocks, which have been dislodged from the overhanging precipices by the effects of frost or convulsions of the elements: in vain do these masses obstruct the progress of the waters of this river. The torrent dashing in cataracts over some of the large boulders and eddying round the base of others, pursues an agitated course until it reaches the desert, through which it glides more calmly, and combines with the Oxus beyond Koollum, whence the confluent waters proceed uninterruptedly to the sea of Aral.

The banks of this river differ from those of the mountain streams in general; they were decked with the most beautiful wild flowers, which bloomed luxuriantly on the bushes, and growing from the deep clefts in the rock, scented the air with their perfume.

The glen is here so filled with large blocks of granite, that to accomplish our passage through it, it was necessary to transfer by manual labour the loads of the baggage animals across the obstructing masses: the difficulties we encountered, and more particularly the romantic scene itself, are still imprinted on my memory.

The wind whistling round the jutting points, the dashing of the waters, and the cries of one of the most timid of our followers, who to save himself from wet feet had mounted an overladen pony, and was now in imminent danger both of Scylla and Charybdis, added to the interest of the picture; but, occasionally, the reverberation caused by the fragments of rock, which, detaching themselves from the upper regions, came tumbling down, not far from where we stood, warned us not to dwell upon the spot. We took the hint, and hastily extricating man and beast, though not until they had experienced a severe ducking, we proceeded onwards to where the waters enclose within their fertilizing arms the grassy fields of the mountain Doaūb. Here it was that we caught the first glimpse of the extensive plains where the Toorkmān mares are turned out to graze; those in foal are left for several months; and after foaling, the animals are put into smaller pastures provided with enclosures, where they are shut up at night. The extent of the larger savannahs is very great, some of them exceeding twenty miles, and the horses that are allowed to range in them become so shy, that their owners only can approach them, and the animals are considered safe from depredators.

As we gradually emerged from the hard bosom of the mountains, we were struck with the simple beauty of this little garden of nature. The vale is triangular, its greatest breadth being about five miles; its whole extent is covered with a rich turf, intermingled by just sufficient cultivated land as to supply the inhabitants with grain. Every wild flower that enlivens our English meads grew here luxuriantly, while the two streams crept along on either side like silver threads bordering a jewelled carpet. This gay and brilliant sight was enhanced by the lofty range of dark frowning hills which encompassed it. It was worthy of being sung as the "Loveliest vale in Toorkisthān."

CHAPTER X.

I have already mentioned that we had received a letter to Shah Pursund Khān, the chief of the Doaūb, who accordingly came out to welcome us to his territory; he embraced us in the Uzbeg fashion, telling us in eastern phraseology "to consider his dominion as our own, and that we might command all he possessed." After many compliments of this nature, he inquired with some bluntness whither we were bound and what our object was? We answered him, that we were proceeding to Koollum, and were anxious to get as much information as he would be good enough to afford us concerning so beautiful a portion of the globe, and we wished to survey its particular features. "Mind," rejoined he, "that the chief of Heibuk and the Meer Walli of Koollum are my enemies, and may be yours." "If," answered Sturt, "we shall meet with the same reception from them as we have hitherto enjoyed from all other chiefs whose possessions we have had occasion to trespass upon during our journeyings, we cannot complain of want of either kindness or hospitality; for as travellers we come, and once eating the 'salt of an Uzbeg,' we know that none would dishonour himself by acting the traitor." "True," retorted the khān, "but he who is your friend while in his dominions will rob you as soon as you set your foot across his frontier." We were not much pleased at this prospect, as we knew he spoke truth when declaring himself at enmity with the surrounding chiefs, but "sufficient for the day is the evil thereof," so we made up our minds to take what advantage we could of his friendly disposition towards us, and trust to our good fortune and the "chapter of accidents" for our future safety. Shah Pursund Khān did not confine his kindness to words, for he sent us an ample supply of flour and clarified butter for our followers, grass and corn for our cattle, and a sheep for ourselves; these sheep are of the Doomba species, with large tails weighing several pounds, which are considered the most delicate part of the animal. He also sent us from his harem an enormous dish of foulādeh, made of wheat boiled to a jelly and strained, and when eaten with sugar and milk palatable and nutritious.

The following morning, as we were preparing to start, I happened to enter into conversation with an aged moollah, the solitary cicerone of the Doaūb, who gave us a brief but very extraordinary account of a cavern about seven miles off; our curiosity was so much excited by the marvellous details we heard, that we determined to delay our departure for the purpose of ascertaining how much of his story was due to the wild imagination of our informant. We accordingly gave orders to unsaddle, and communicated our intentions to the khan. At first he strongly urged us not to put our plan into execution, declaring that the cave was the domicile of the evil one, and that no stranger who had presumed to intrude upon the privacy of the awful inhabitant had ever returned to tell of what he had seen. It will easily be imagined that these warnings only made us more determined upon visiting the spot. At length, finding our resolution immovable, the khān, much to our astonishment, declared that it was not from personal fear, but from anxiety for our safety that he had endeavoured to deter us, but that, as we were obstinate, he would at least afford us the advantage of his protection, and accompany us, I confess we were not sanguine in our expectations that he would keep his word, and were not a little surprised to see him shortly after issue forth from his fort fully armed, and accompanied by his principal followers. We immediately made all necessary preparations, and started on our visit to his satanic majesty.

A bridle-path conducted us for some miles along the edge of a gentle stream, whose banks were clothed with long luxuriant grass extending on either side for a few hundred yards; we proceeded rapidly at first, keeping our horses at a hand gallop, as the path was smooth, and also to escape from the myriads of forest-flies or bloodsuckers which were perpetually hovering around us, and irritating our cattle almost to madness whenever we were obliged to slacken our pace; our tormentors, however, did not pursue us beyond the limits of the pasture land, so that we were glad to exchange the beauties of the prairie for the stony barren ground which succeeded it. We soon reached the base of a hill from whence the wished-for cavern was visible, situated about half-way up its face. We were now obliged to dismount, and leaving our horses under the charge of an Uzbeg, who could hardly conceal his delight at being selected for the least dangerous duty, we commenced the ascent.

During our ride I had endeavoured to gather a few more particulars concerning the dreaded cavern, and as might have been expected, the anticipated horrors dwindled away considerably as we approached it; still enough of the marvellous remained to keep my curiosity on the stretch. Shah Pursund Khān confessed that he was not positive that the devil actually lived there, but still, he said, it was very probable; he had first heard of the existence of the cave when he obtained possession of the Doāub twelve years ago, from the very moollah who was our informant. Urged by a curiosity similar to our own, he had ventured some little distance inside, but suddenly he came upon the print of a naked foot, and beside it another extraordinary impression, which he suspected to be from the foot of sheittan (the devil) himself; quite satisfied that he had gone far enough, he retreated precipitately, and from that day to this had never intruded again. He argued that any *human* being living in the cave would require sustenance, and of course would purchase it at his fort, which was the only one where the necessaries of life could be procured for many miles around; but he knew every one who came to him, and no stranger had ever come on such an errand; he therefore concluded with an appealing look to the moollah who was with us. The moollah, however, had a tale of his own to tell, and seemed to have no great respect for the superstitious fears of his patron. "The name of the cavern is Yeermālik, and the fact of the matter is this," said he, settling himself in his saddle for a long story. "In the time of the invasion, six hundred years ago, of Genghis Khān the Tartar, seven hundred men of the Huzareh tribe, with their wives and families and a stock of provisions, took possession of this cavern, hoping to escape the fury of the ruthless invader, and never stirred beyond its mouth. But the cruel Genghis, after wasting the country with fire and sword, set on foot a strict search for such of the unfortunate inhabitants as had fled from his tyranny. His bloodhounds soon scented the wretched Huzarehs, and a strong party was sent to drive them from their place of refuge. But despair lent to the besieged a courage which was not the characteristic of their tribe, and knowing that, if taken alive, a lingering torture and cruel death would be their fate, they resolved to make good their defence at every hazard. The mouth of the cave was small, and no sooner did the invaders rush in than they were cut down by those inside; in vain were more men thrust in to take the place of those slain; the advantages of position were too great, and they were obliged at length to desist. But Genghis was not to be balked of his victims, and his devilish cunning suggested the expedient of lighting straw at the mouth of the cave to suffocate those inside, but the size of the place prevented his plan from taking effect; so he at last commanded a large fragment of rock to be rolled to the mouth of the cavern, adding another as a support, and having thus effectually barred their exit, he cruelly abandoned them to their fate. Of course the whole party suffered a miserable death, and it is perhaps the spirits of the murdered men that, wandering about and haunting it, have given a suspicious character to the place; but," concluded he, rather dogmatically, "the devil *does not* live there now--it is too cold!!"[*]

[* Note: Those who have been familiarized to the atrocities perpetrated by the French in Algeria will not feel the horror that the moollah's tale would otherwise have excited; the similarity of these outrages to humanity is so striking, that I quote a passage extracted from the French paper, "The National," which will speak for itself.

"The National gives a frightful picture of Marshal Bugeaud's doings in Africa. According to the accounts published by this paper, fifty prisoners were one day shot in cold blood--thirteen villages burned--the Dahra massacre acted over again, for it appears that a portion of a tribe having hid themselves in a cave, the same means were resorted to exactly as those employed by Colonel Pelissier, and all smoked and baked to death. The Marshal himself is the author of all these horrors--his last triumph was a monster razzia--he has ordered the most strict secrecy as to his barbarous proceedings; and the writer of the accounts calls him a second Attila, for he puts all to the sword and fire, sparing only women and children."]

After scrambling over loose stones, climbing up precipices, and crawling round the projecting rocks, which consumed an hour, we found ourselves on a small ledge in front of the outer aperture, which was nearly circular and about fifty feet high. We were now in a cavern apparently of no great extent, and as I could not discover any other passage, I began to fancy that it was for this paltry hole we had undergone so much fatigue, and had had our expectations raised so high. I was about to give utterance to my disappointment, when I perceived the Uzbegs preparing their torches and arranging the line of march, in which it seemed that no one was anxious to take precedence. I now began to look about me, in the hope that there was something more to be seen, and was delighted to observe one adventurous hero with a torch disappear behind some masses of rock. We all followed our leader, and it was with great difficulty that, one by one, we managed to squeeze ourselves through a narrow gap between two jagged rocks, which I presume I am to consider as the identical ones that were rolled to the mouth six hundred years ago at the stern command of the Tartar Attila.

I confess that hitherto I had treated the moollah's account as an idle tale; my unbelief, however, was quickly removed, for just as we entered the narrow passage the light of the torches was for an instant thrown upon a group of human skeletons. I saw them but for an instant, and the sight was quite sufficient to raise my drooping curiosity to its former pitch.

View of the Outer Cave of Yeermallik, shewing the Entrance Hole to the larger Cavern

Drawn by Mr Gempertz
Pelham Richardson Litho

CHAPTER XI.

We proceeded down the sloping shaft, occasionally bruising ourselves against its jagged sides, until our leader suddenly came to a dead halt. I was next to him, and coming up as close as I could, I found that one step further would have precipitated the adventurous guide into an abyss, the bottom and sides of which were undistinguishable; after gazing for a moment into this apparently insurmountable obstacle to our further progress, I could just perceive a narrow ledge about sixteen feet below me, that the eye could trace for a few yards only, beyond which it was lost in the deep gloom surrounding us. Our conductor had already made up his mind what to do: he proceeded to unwind his long narrow turban composed of cotton cloth, and called to his comrades to do the same; by joining these together they formed a kind of rope by means of which we gradually lowered each other, till at last a party ten in number were safely landed on the ledge. We left a couple of men to haul us up on our return, and proceeded on our way, groping along the brink of the yawning chasm. Every now and then loose stones set in motion by our feet would slip into this bottomless pit, and we could hear them bounding down from ledge to ledge, smashing themselves into a thousand fragments, till the echoes so often repeated were like the independent file-firing of a battalion of infantry. Sometimes the narrow path would be covered for a distance of many feet with a smooth coat of ice, and then it was indeed dangerous. After moving on in this way for some minutes, the road gradually widened till we found ourselves on the damp and dripping flooring of a chamber of unknown dimensions; the torch light was not strong enough to enable us to conceive the size of this subterraneous hall, but all around us lay scattered melancholy proofs that there was some sad foundation for the moollah's story. Hundreds of human skeletons were strewed around; as far as the eye could penetrate these mournful relics presented themselves; they were very perfect, and had evidently not been disturbed since death; some had more the appearance of the shrivelled-up remains which we find in the Morgue on the road to the Grand St. Bernard, and lay about us in all the varied positions induced by their miserable fate. Here, it seemed that a group had, while sufficient strength yet remained, huddled themselves together, as if to keep up the vital warmth of which death so slowly and yet so surely was depriving them; a little farther on was a figure in a sitting posture, with two infants still clasped in its bony arms; and then again the eye would fall upon some solitary figure with outstretched limbs, as if courting that death which on the instant responded to the call.

Involuntarily my thoughts recurred to Dante's beautiful description of the Comte Ugolino's children and their piteous end in the Torre della Fame--but here, a sickening sense of the dreadful reality of the horrors, which it was evident from these mute memorials of man's cruelty to his fellow had been endured, quite oppressed me, and I wished I had never visited the spot. I felt myself so much harrowed by this sad scene, that I endeavoured to distract my attention; but what was my astonishment when my eye fell upon the print of a human naked foot, and beside it the distinct mark of the pointed heel of the Affghān boot!--I hope my reader will give me credit for truth--I can assure him that it was some time before I could believe my own eyes, though I considered that the result of our explorations would explain in part the sight, which appeared to me so extraordinary, and which tallied so strangely with the footprints which had frightened Shah Pursund Khan twelve years ago. I was still absorbed in reflections of no very gay colour, when one of the attendants warned me that if I staid all day amongst the "dead people," there would not be sufficient oil to feed the torches, and we should be unable to visit the Ice Caves. I was immediately roused, and proceeded onwards with the party through several low arches and smaller caves,--suddenly a strange glare spread itself about me, and after a few more steps a magnificent spectacle presented itself. In the centre of a large cave stood an enormous mass of clear ice, smooth and polished as a mirror, and in the form of a gigantic beehive, with its dome-shaped top just touching the long icicles which depended from the jagged surface of the rock. A small aperture led to the interior of this wonderful congelation, the walls of which were nearly two feet thick--the floor, sides, and roof were smooth and slippery, and our figures were reflected from floor to ceiling and from side to side in endless repetition. The inside of this chilly abode was divided into several compartments of every fantastic shape; in some the glittering icicles hung like curtains from the roof; in others the vault was smooth as glass. Beautifully brilliant were the prismatic colours reflected from the varied surface of the ice, when the torches flashed suddenly upon them as we passed from cave to cave. Around, above, beneath, every thing was of solid ice, and being unable to stand on account of its slippery nature, we slid or rather glided mysteriously along the glassy surface of this hall of spells. In one of the largest compartments the icicles had reached the floor, and gave the idea of pillars supporting the roof. Altogether the sight was to me as novel as it was magnificent, and I only regret that my powers of description are inadequate to do justice to what I saw.

View of
the Ice
Caves
in the Cav-
ern of
Yeermallik

Drawn by
Mr Gem-
pertz
Pelham
Richardson
Litho

After wandering for some time amongst these extraordinary chambers, we proceeded further to examine the nature of the caverns in which they were formed: these seemed to branch out into innumerable galleries, which again intersected each other. Sometimes they expanded into halls, the dimensions of which our feeble light prevented us from calculating, and anon they contracted into narrow passages, so low that we were obliged to creep along them on our hands and knees. Our party had just emerged from one of these defiles and were standing together on a kind of sloping platform, at which point the declivity seemed to become more precipitous as it receded from our sight, when our attention was suddenly arrested by the reappearance of the mysterious naked footprints which I had before observed in the chamber of skeletons. I examined them minutely, and am certain from the spread of the toes that they belonged to some one who was in the habit of going barefoot. I took a torch, and determined to trace them as far as I could. Had I met with these prints in the open air, I should have decided upon their being quite fresh, but the even temperature and stillness of atmosphere which reigned in these strange regions might account for the tracks retaining that sharpness of outline which denotes a recent impression. The direction I took led me immediately down the slope I have just mentioned, and its increasing steepness caused me some misgivings as to how I should get back, when suddenly a large stone on which I had rested my foot gave way beneath my weight, and down I came, extinguishing my torch in my fall. Luckily I managed to stop myself from rolling down the fearful chasm which yawned beneath, but the heavy rounded fragment of rock rolled onwards, first with a harsh grating sound, as if it reluctantly quitted its resting place, then, gradually acquiring impetus, down it thundered, striking against other rocks and dragging them on with it, till the loud echoes repeated a thousand times from the distant caves mingling with the original sound raised a tumult of noise quite sufficient to scare a braver crew than our party consisted of. The effect of my mishap was instantaneous. Our followers raised an universal shout of Sheitān, Sheitān, (the devil, the devil,) and rushed helter skelter back from the direction of the sound. In the confusion all the torches carried by the natives were extinguished, and had not my friend Sturt displayed the most perfect coolness and self-possession, we should have been in an alarming predicament; for he (uninfluenced by any such supernatural fears as had been excited amongst the runaways by the infernal turmoil produced by my unlucky foot, and though himself ignorant of the cause of it from having been intent upon the footmarks when I slipped), remained perfectly unmoved with his torch, the only one still burning, raised high above his head, waiting patiently till the panic should subside. Order was at length restored in some degree, but the thirst of enterprise was cooled, and the natives loudly declared they would follow the devil no farther, and that we must return forthwith. Shah Pursund Khān, who was just as great a coward as the rest, declared it was no use following the track any more, for it was well known the cavern extended to Cabul!!! Finding it useless endeavouring to revive the broken spirits of these cravens, we reluctantly commenced a retrograde movement, and I was obliged to remain in lasting ignorance of the nature of the mysterious origin of the footprint.

We had considerable difficulty in finding our way back to the ice rooms; the fears of our followers had now completely got the better of them; they lost their presence of mind, and, consequently, their way; and it was not till after we had wandered about for more than an hour that we hit upon the ledge which eventually led us to the drop which we had originally descended by means of the ladder of turbans. At the head of this drop we had left a couple of men to haul us up; as soon as they perceived the light of our expiring torches, they called out loudly to us to make haste and get out of the place, for they had seen the *Sheitān*, about an hour ago, run along the ledge beneath them, and disappear in the gloom beyond. This information raised the terror of the poor natives to a climax; all made a rush for the rope of turbans, and four or five having clutched hold of it, were in the act of dragging down turban, men, and torches upon our devoted heads, when Sturt interfered, and by his firm remonstrances, aided by the timely fall of a few well-aimed stones upon the heads of the crew, made them relax their grasp and ascend one by one.

The chief, being the lightest, claimed the privilege of being drawn up first, which was readily agreed to; and so in succession each when he had mounted assisted in drawing up his companions, till at last we were all safely landed at the top, out of the reach of *any ordinary sized* devil. We soon emerged into the open air, covered with dust from head to foot like Indian Faqueers, after having been for nearly four hours wandering in the bowels of the earth. Our followers soon regained their courage now that the danger was past, and each in turn began to boast of his own valour and sneer at the pusillanimity of his comrade; but all agreed that nothing on earth or in heaven should ever tempt them again to visit the ice-caves of Yeermallick.

CHAPTER XII.

On the 13th of July we bade adieu to our friend Shah Pursund Khān, who accompanied us a short distance on our way, after in vain endeavouring to induce us to remain with him for some time longer, this we could not accede to, but promised, if our time permitted, to pay him a lengthened visit on our return. We had a long march this day, the distance being nearly eighteen miles; but our beasts of burden were much the better for their day's halt, and, the greater part of the road being a descent, we reached Rhoeh, where we pitched our tents, in very good time. The first few miles were along the delightful valley of the Doaub, which we reluctantly quitted, and after crossing a low ridge descended through broken country till we reached the foot of the hills, where I observed for the first time a genuine Tartar krail, composed of a number of small black blanket tents fastened to a kind of wattle. In the plain of Rhoeh is a small mud fort in a dilapidated state, and uninhabited; the village itself was not of any importance, the habits of the people being evidently migratory.

The Jerboa is a native of this country as well as the steppes of Tartary, where it is most commonly found in the shrubless plains; in form it is a miniature of the kangaroo, to which in some of its peculiarities it bears a close resemblance, though in size it is very little larger than our common English rat. The name of the "Vaulting Rat," by which it is known among naturalists, is very applicable. These little animals burrow deeply in the ground, and the method of dislodging them adopted by us was the pouring a quantity of water into their holes, which causes them to rush out at another aperture, when they commence leaping about in a surprising manner until they observe another burrow and instantly disappear. If chased, they spring from the hind quarters, darting about here and there, and affording great amusement to the pursuers. It is difficult to hold them, as they are rarely grasped without losing a portion of their long and beautiful tails. The forelegs are much shorter than the hind ones, the ears are very large and silky, and the eye surpassingly black and brilliant. It is a harmless animal, and no doubt when tamed would be perfectly domesticated.

Nothing of interest occurred either this day or the next, which brought us, after another dreary march of seventeen miles, to the fort and village of Koorrum. For nearly the whole distance between Rhoeh and Koorrum not a drop of water is procurable; as we had not provided against this contingency, we suffered in proportion. Altogether this part of the road offers considerable obstacles to the progress of an army, from its numerous ravines and steep though short ascents and descents, which would be very difficult for artillery; I should, from a cursory glance at the country, imagine that these steep pitches might be avoided by a more circuitous route, though the one we pursued was the beaten track for the caravans, and they generally find out the most convenient passage. The approach to Koorrum was pretty, but the scenery was of a character with which we were now so familiar that its peculiar beauties did not perhaps impress us as much as when they afforded the additional charm of novelty. A succession of walnut, apricot, mulberry, and apple trees shaded our path, which lay through extensive orchards, carpeted with beautiful turf. The vines clung to the sycamore trees; and where the spade had been at work, corn and artificial grasses grew in abundance. Our next halting place was Sarbagh, where we arrived on the 15th, after marching through a pleasant and fruitful valley, flanked by parallel belts of mountain land, the agreeable verdure relieving the eye from the barrenness of this, I may call it, parietal range. The ornamental trees which fringe the banks of the Koollum river, as it gracefully pursues its course to the Oxus, had altogether a very picturesque appearance.

The son of Baber Beg, the chief of Heibuk, was at this time residing at Sarbagh, and shewed us every possible attention, sending us sheep, fowls, corn, flour, fruit, and every article required for about seventy people. It was very gratifying to us to find that we were treated by the Uzbeg chiefs in so friendly a manner, as we had some misgivings lest our being unprovided with any letters from influential men in Cābul, might create unfavourable surmises amongst a half-savage and naturally suspicious race. Doubtless we gained a large portion of attention and civility from the idea which pervaded all our hosts that we were great hakeems, *physicians*, and if we chose, could relieve the human body from every illness whether real or imaginary––and I was glad to remark that the latter class of ailment was by far the most common. Still, some diseases were very prevalent, particularly those which may be considered as induced by a total absence of cleanliness. Sore eyes were very common here, as in Affghanistān, and our powers and medicine chest were sometimes rather too severely taxed by importunate applicants, who never would apply the remedy in the manner described, unless it was administered upon principles which they understood, and which was in accordance with their own reasoning. In Cābul, the medical officers were the only class of Europeans allowed an entrance to the harems of the rich, when they were expected after feeling the pulse of some Cashmerian beauty to pronounce her malady, and effect her cure forthwith. The lords of the creation too, debilitated from early dissipation or a life of debauchery, sued for remedies and charms, which, alas! are only to be found in the hundredth edition of a work known by its mysterious advertisement in the columns of a London newspaper.

On the 16th, after a long march of twenty-two miles, we approached Heibuk through the same kind of scenery as the preceding day; on rounding a projecting ledge of rock we saw that fortress in the distance, on an insulated eminence adjacent to a low range of hills. Meer Baber Beg has placed his fortress in a very respectable state of defence, quite adequate to repel the desultory inroads of his predatory neighbours; but commanded by and exposed to enfilade from the hills about it, on one of these hills he has built a tower as a kind of outwork, but it is very weak and of insignificant size.

The only thing worth seeing near Heibuk is the Tukt-i-Rustum or Throne of Hercules, which we accordingly visited, and found it to be a fortification of no very great extent on a most uncommon principle, and of unknown date. The best idea I can convey to the reader of its shape, is by begging him to cut an orange in half, and place its flat surface in a saucer; he will then have a tolerable model of the Tukt-i-Rustum. We entered by a narrow gallery piercing through the solid mass of rock which forms the outer wall or saucer, and leading by an irregular flight of steps to the summit of the orange. I instituted many enquiries concerning the origin of this place, but I could obtain no information; not even a legend beyond that it was holy. We were accompanied by one of the chief's sons, a fat jolly youth of about four-and-twenty, with a countenance that was a type of his good humour--he sat with us for some time whilst we were at our toilette, but affected to be somewhat shocked at the very scanty clothing which we considered sufficient while our Bheesties poured the contents of their mussocks[*] over us. It was rather amusing to hear the remarks of the bystanders, who seemed to view cleanliness as a consideration very secondary to etiquette. It would have been fortunate for us if I could have persuaded our criticising friends to try on their own persons the advantage of a dash of fresh water, for they were without exception the most filthy race it has ever been my misfortune to meet; their garments teem with life, and sometimes, after merely sitting on the same rug placed to receive visitors, I have been under the necessity of making a fresh toilette.

[* Note: Skins of water.]

Meer Baber Beg was a great man in these parts, and kindly sent us three sheep, with fowls, flour, fruits, and grain in abundance, intimating, at the same time, his intention to pay us a visit in the evening. He came accordingly, and favoured us with his presence for a considerable time. He seemed an intelligent man, but in a very infirm state of health, and quite crippled from rheumatism. One would hardly have supposed, while admiring his pleasing features, which expressed so much benignity, that when on the throne of Koollum he had been such a bloody tyrant; yet such was the case;-- though the hereditary ruler of Koollum and its dependencies, he had by his brutality made himself so obnoxious, that he was deposed by his own subjects headed by his younger brother, and dare not now shew his face on his paternal estate.

This corpulent son whom I have before mentioned brought a double-barrelled percussion gun for my inspection, and requested that I would test its qualities on some pigeons that were flying about; I was fortunate enough to bring down a couple on the wing, but was somewhat mortified to find that the burst of admiration which followed my feat was entirely confined to the weapon, which, together with the donor, Dr. Lord, was praised to the skies, whilst no kind of credit was given to my skill in using it.

We halted at Heibuk on the 17th, as the Meer requested we would stay a day with him before putting ourselves in the power of the dreaded Meer Walli of Koollum. At first he endeavoured to persuade us to abandon our project of proceeding further, but, finding us determined, he contented himself with relating every possible story he could remember or invent concerning the many acts of cruel treachery which the Meer Walli had perpetrated, and concluded by an eulogium on his own manifold virtues.

During the course of the day a Hindoo from Peshawur peeped cautiously into my tent, and, on my inquiring his business, he approached, and with many salaams, laid a bag of money at my feet; rather astonished at so unusual an offering, I requested to know the cause of this act of generosity, and I was informed that it was a "first offering," or, in other words, a bribe to propitiate me, in the hope that I would use my influence to get the Hindoo out of the clutches of Meer Baber Beg. The story he told me was, that some years back he came to Heibuk to trade, and having made a little money was packing up his property preparatory to his departure, when he was suddenly ordered into the Meer's presence. "Friend," said this benign ruler, "stay here a little longer; it is not right that, having made a sum of money in my country, you should spend it in your own." Since then, he added, he had been ill-treated and robbed several times to satisfy the rapacity of this wicked monster; and then, as if frightened at his own expressions, he peered cautiously round the tent, apparently fancying the Meer himself would start from behind the screen to punish him for his audacity. I returned him his 250 rupees, but told him if his story were true I would use what little influence I possessed to procure his release. When Baber Beg came to pay us his evening visit I broached the subject, and requested as a favour that the Hindoo might be permitted to accompany our party as a guide and interpreter. "If you will take my advice," said he, "you will have nothing to say to the scoundrel, who will come to a bad end: he has been deceiving you; but if, after my warning, you still wish to have him as a guide, take him by all means."

Accordingly I took him, but in justice to the Meer's discrimination of character it must be owned that my protegé, as soon as he considered himself safe from the Meer's indignation, proved himself to the full as great a scoundrel as he had been represented. The following morning, before taking our departure, Start presented to the Meer's youngest son a handsome pair of percussion pistols, for which the father seemed so very grateful that I could not help suspecting he intended to appropriate them to his own use as soon as we were well away.

On leaving the fortress of Heibuk we passed through a very extensive cultivated district, the principal produce being the grain which in Hindoostan is called jowār. The remaining portion of our journey to Hazree Sooltān, which was a distance of eighteen miles, was nothing but a barren waste with occasional patches of low jungle. We were now evidently on the farthest spur of the Hindoo Khoosh; the hills were low and detached, gradually uniting into the endless plain which bounded the horizon to the north and west. On the road we met a messenger who was on his way to Sir Alexander Burnes at Kābul, having come from Bokhara, bearing a letter from the *Vakeel*, or native ambassador, whom Sir Alexander had sent some time back to endeavour, by persuasion or stratagem, to effect the release of our unfortunate countryman, Col. Stoddart. The courier, who had received the account from the Vakeel, whether true or false he could not inform us, stated "that Col. Stoddart accompanied the Persian army to Herāt, and finding they could not make the desired impression on the walls, raised the siege, and the Colonel left the army and proceeded across to Bokhara, whether to endeavour to effect the release of the Russian slaves, (there being many in the dominions of the Bokhara King,) or merely for amusement, he could not say; but that the latter was the generally received opinion. On approaching the city of the tyrant king he met a man riding furiously away with a woman, and as she passed, called out to the Colonel Amaun, Amaun! mercy, mercy! whereupon he immediately galloped up to the ravisher, and securing the deliverance of the woman, told her to keep under his protection until he entered the city. On the first day after his arrival the King passed as the Colonel was riding on horseback, and although the latter gave the salute usual in his own country, it did not satisfy the ruler; moreover, he, the Feringhi, was on horseback without permission, and therefore the Khan ordered him the following day into his presence. Messengers the next morning were sent, who abruptly entered the Colonel's house, and finding he would not willingly submit, dragged him before their chief. He was asked, why he had infringed the customs of the country by riding on horseback in the city, and why he did not pay the recognised submission to the ruler of a free country? The reply was, that the same compliment had been paid to the King of Bokhara as was customary in Europe to a crowned head. And why have you presumed to ride on horseback within the city walls, where no Feringhi is allowed? Because I was ignorant of the custom. It's a lie; my messengers ordered you to dismount and you would not. 'Tis true, they did order me and I did not, but I thought they were doing more than their duty. After this the King ordered him into confinement, where he now is."

The courier, after giving us this information, remarked that he was penniless, and that as his business concerned the safety of a countryman, he hoped we would assist him. Though we were not quite satisfied with the man's story, we stood the chance of its being true, and furnished him with funds for the prosecution of his journey, for which, on our return to Cabul, we were kindly thanked by Sir Alexander, who informed us that the note from the Vakeel conveyed the intelligence of the failure of his endeavours, and that he had himself been put in confinement.

At the time of which I am writing both Dost Mahommed Khān and his notorious son Akbar were prisoners at Bokhara; but the means taken by *their* friends to release them were more successful than those adopted by our politicals at Cabul. It appears that the chief at Shere Subz had for some time been at enmity with his Bokhara neighbour, and, wishing to do Dost Mahommed a good turn, he picked out fifty of the most expert thieves in his dominions--a difficult selection where the claims of all to this bad preeminence were so strong--but the Shere Subz chief was from experience a tolerable judge of the qualifications of an expert rogue, and having pitched upon his men, he promised them valuable presents, provided they effected, by whatever means they might choose to adopt, the release of the Dost; hinting at the same time that if they failed he should be under the necessity of seizing and selling their families. The thieves were successful, and at the expiration of a month the Dost was free.

If we could have interested the chief of Shere Subz in our favour by presents and fair words, might not the same means have been employed for the rescue of poor Stoddart? The only way to deal with a ruffian like him of Bokhara would have been by pitting against him some of his own stamp.

The King of Bokhara has several times endeavoured to coerce the Shere Subz's chief, but the instant a hostile force appears on his frontiers, the latter causes the whole of his country to be inundated, so that the invader is obliged to retire, and is by this stratagem kept at a respectful distance.

Another traveller came across us this day, who had resided for some years at Kokān, and furnished us with some account of the nature of the Chinese garrison of that fort. It is situated on an isolated rock, and every five years relieved with men, provisions, and ammunition; the flanks of the bastions are armed with ponderous wall pieces, requiring three men to work them. Chambers are also bored in the live rock, from whence enormous masses of stone might be discharged on an assailing foe. The Kokānese have often attempted to dislodge the intruders, but owing to the good state of defence in which the fort is kept, and the strong escorts under which the reliefs are regularly forwarded, they have been always repulsed with severe loss. My informant had been in the service of the Kokānese, and was now on his way to Hindoostan; in military notions he must have been of the famous Captain Dugald Dalgetty's school, for I afterwards met him as a non-commissioned officer in Shah Seujah's Goorkah battalion.

CHAPTER XIII.

A march of eighteen miles brought us on the 19th July to Koollum. The road continued along the banks of the river, through a wide valley bounded by low distant hills for nearly the whole way. Towards the end of our journey a spur from these hills struck right across the direction of the river, which had forced for itself a passage through the obstacle without deviating much from its rectilinear course, but considerably disturbing its previously placid character, for here it rushed with impetuous violence through the narrow cleft which it had formed, through this, the most advanced outpost of the glorious range of the Hindoo Khoosh. The defile, though short, was difficult of access and capable of being long defended; there is a small tower about the centre, slightly removed from and commanding the road: but a mere handfull of troops stationed on the crags above could, by hurling down the loosened masses of rock which totter on the edge of the cliff, for a time effectually stop the progress of a hostile army from either side. I should imagine, however, that this as well as every other pass I have ever seen except the Khyber and Bolun would be more easily turned than forced. On emerging from this last defile, a prospect presents itself strongly contrasting with the romantic scenery we had recently been witnessing. Immediately before us lay the populous city of Koollum, the fortress standing on a small isolated eminence, and the dome-shaped houses embosomed in the deep foliage of their gardens and orchards clustered round it for miles on every side. Immediately on the outskirts of the city the desert commences, which, stretching away to Bokhara as far as the eye could reach, formed a melancholy and uninviting background to the busy scene before us. As we approached the city, we had our misgivings as to the nature of our reception by the Meer Walli, as, contrary to the treatment we had invariably experienced from the chiefs of all the considerable places through which we had had occasion to pass since entering Toorkisthān, no one appeared on the part of the Meer to welcome us. At length, after wandering about the suburbs for more than an hour, followed by a crowd of gaping idlers who seemed half disposed to question our right of *squatting*, we selected an open space and commenced unloading our baggage animals, and prepared to establish ourselves.

View of Koollum, from the eastward.

Drawn by J. Cowell Esq!! Pelham Richardso Litho

Our spirits were raised, however, soon after, by the welcome arrival of an officer of the Meer's household, who was sent by his master to convey us to the caravanserai, where, after a short period, we received three or four sheep with fruit and other provisions of all descriptions, which supply was regularly continued during the whole time we remained at Koollum. Our uneasiness, thus quieted, was soon entirely dispelled by a message announcing that a visit from the great man himself would take place in the evening. We must have been rather difficult to please, however, on this particular day, for after the wished-for visit was over, we both agreed that it had been dreadfully tiresome; to be sure, as fate would have it, we had not had time to eat our dinner before his arrival, and etiquette obliged us to defer eating till after his departure, which did not release us till past midnight, though he made his appearance soon after eight o'clock.

In person the Meer Walli was certainly very prepossessing; his voice was peculiarly musical, and his manner gentlemanly and easy; his face would have been eminently handsome but for a dreadful wound by which he had lost a portion of his nose. At this our first interview nothing relative to our own future proceedings was discussed, though that was the subject uppermost in our own minds, as we could not but feel ourselves entirely at the mercy of a robber prince of notorious character. As it was, the conversation was made up of those compliments and common-places with which the Orientals know so well how to fill up "awkward pauses," when, for reasons of their own, they do not intend talking upon the real business. He very politely acceded to our request of visiting the bazaar the following morning, which being market-day, the influx of strangers from the Tartar encampments at the different oases of the Bokhara Desert, and country people from the Toorkisthān mountains, was very great. One of his household was always in attendance as we passed out of the gate of the caravanserai, where we lodged, to conduct us about, and act in the double capacity of spy and cicerone. The city was crowded, and our appearance excited considerable sensation––much more so in truth than was pleasant, for we were followed wherever we went by a very curious and a very dirty crowd. We had heard a good deal about the Mahommedan college at Koollum, and of course were very anxious to see what comparison existed between it and our own colleges: we could trace none beyond the term of college. The house itself was new and capacious, with clean-looking apartments for the scholars. We entered the halls of study, which were long narrow verandahs, and found several white-bearded and sagacious-looking Moollahs reading out portions of the Korān to their attentive scholars, with a grave countenance and a loud nasal twang, exciting a propensity to laughter which I with difficulty repressed. I do not think the reasoning of the college is very deep, or that the talents of its senior wrangler need be very first-rate, and am inclined to suspect that this pompous reading was got up for the occasion for the purpose of astonishing the weak intellects of the Feringhee strangers.

From the college we proceeded to the slave market, which was well furnished, and chiefly supplied from the ever victimized Huzarehs; the women were generally ill-favoured, but all appeared contented with their lot so that *somebody* purchased them. After making the tour of the city in search of wonders, we returned home, hot, wearied, and disappointed, for we had found nothing to repay us for the annoyances we had been subjected to from the impertinent curiosity of the filthy multitude. Our own intentions were to get away from Koollum in order to be able to reach Balkh and return to Cābul before the cold weather should set in; but alas! our wishes were not destined to be fulfilled. Our uneasiness concerning the real intentions of the Meer was again excited towards the evening, for one of our followers came to us almost frantic with terror, stammering out as soon as his nervous state permitted him to speak, that he had heard it stated as a notorious fact that we were all to be detained at Koollum––that such was the pleasure of the Meer. The reader will believe that this intelligence was any thing but satisfactory; I could not help conjuring up visions of a long and wearisome captivity––of hope deferred and expectations disappointed––with Stoddart's melancholy situation as a near precedent. I managed to make myself for a short time as thoroughly uncomfortable as if I were already a prisoner, but soon a sense of the great foolishness of indulging in this tone of thought came over me, and making a strong effort to shake off the gloomy shadows of an imaginary future, I betook myself to consider the best means of ascertaining, in the first instance, the truth of the report, which if I had done so at once would have saved me a good deal of painful thought. As a preliminary step I desired a couple of our Affghān escort to proceed, so as not to excite suspicion, to the bourj or *watch tower* in the centre of the defile by which we had approached Koollum, and through which our only retreat must have been, to ascertain if the post was occupied by any of the Meer's people. They soon brought us the satisfactory intelligence that not a man was to be seen; but the Affghāns qualified their information by persisting in their opinion that some treachery was intended. So strong was this feeling amongst our men that it became imperatively necessary that our doubts should be resolved into certainty one way or the other, and Sturt and I, after a short consultation, determined that at the interview which was to take place next morning we should put the question to the chief categorically. Having come to this conclusion, we were obliged to smoke the "pipe of patience" on the "couch of uncertainty" till the Meer Walli arrived.

The Meer made his appearance the following morning, and, after the usual compliments, to our great astonishment himself touched on the subject. "I have heard," said he, "that you have sent out spies to see if the Bourj in the defile is occupied, and if any of my people are abroad to restrain your movements." This was rather an ominous commencement: "but," continued the old gentleman, "if such had been my intention, could I not have put the whole of you into confinement the moment you arrived? At all events, what could you and your party do against my force?" Sturt glanced his eye at the speaker; for an instant, too, it rested on me, as if to read my opinion; then he boldly answered, "You may outnumber us by thousands, but you will never capture us alive." He said this so calmly, with such politeness of manner, and yet so firmly, that the Meer was evidently taken aback: at length he replied, "But no such piece of villainy has ever entered my head." He then adroitly changed the subject, and shortly after took his leave.

When he was gone we held another council of war. It was by no means clear that the last declaration of the chief was a sincere one; but it might have been a temporizing answer elicited by the perhaps unexpected boldness of Sturt's remark. We determined, at all events, to keep on the alert, guard against any surprise, avoid as much as possible offering any pretext for offence, and, if the worst came to the worst, make as good a resistance as we could.

The next day we received a polite message, requesting an interview, and asking us to visit him in his favourite garden. Under all circumstances we deemed it best to allow it to appear that our suspicions were dissipated, and we accordingly accepted the invitation, and found the Meer seated on the chabooka, or *raised platform of masonry*, under the shade of some magnificent trees. He immediately commenced saying, "The reason I did not go out to meet you as you approached my city is, that during the warm weather I sleep the greater portion of the day and sit up enjoying the coolness of the night air; but I sent a messenger to escort you in with all care, and unfortunately *he missed the way*." Such an excuse was possible, but not at all probable. We did not give him credit for telling the truth about the guide, as there was only one road from Heibuk, and the approach of our party to Koollum was known in the city several days before our arrival. It was now evident to us that on our approach the Meer Walli was undecided whether he should treat us as friends or foes; it seemed that for the present he had determined in our favour, but distrusting his capricious disposition we were only the more anxious to get out of his reach, though we both agreed that the wisest and safest plan would be to carry our heads very high and put a bold front upon all our proceedings. This decision we came to whilst sitting in the garden in the presence of the Meer. Suddenly we heard a confused murmur behind us, and the heavy sound of the butt end of several muskets striking the ground as in "ordering arms;" we turned sharply round, and perceived with astonishment, not unmingled with satisfaction, that six or eight of our Affghān guard, notwithstanding the numerous followers round the Meer, had entered the garden of their own accord and placed themselves immediately in our rear with bayonets fixed. The Meer appeared to take no notice of this extraordinary intrusion, and after a few compliments permitted us to withdraw.

On returning to the caravanserai we inquired why the guard had acted thus without orders; they told us they had secretly heard that treachery was intended by the Meer towards us, and that therefore they had deemed it their duty to protect us from any surprise; moreover, that ten more of the guard had been stationed close outside the garden ready to support them at a moment's notice. Our own opinion was that at that time nothing of the kind was in contemplation, but it was satisfactory to view the determined spirit which animated our men. Strange anomaly that these very men who now came voluntarily forward to protect our persons from insult at the imminent risk of their lives, should have been found amongst those who, with their arms and accoutrements, had deserted in a body from the British to the side of the Ex-Ameer at the battle of Bameeān a few months after.

CHAPTER XIV.

Pursuant to our plan of appearing to have full confidence in the Meer Walli's integrity of purpose, we affected to lay aside all personal precaution and courted his society, of which, to say truth, he seemed disposed to give us plenty. We had several interviews with him,--indeed, hardly a day passed without his sending for and honouring us with his presence for several hours.

During these meetings we used every endeavour to sound the chief as to his intentions with respect to us, without betraying an undue anxiety on the subject, but could make very little out of him.

Our conversation frequently turned on military matter, and many very pertinent questions were put to us relative to our rank, pay, duties, discipline, &c. On Sturt informing him that he was in the engineer department, and that his particular duties were to construct bridges, repair fortifications, superintend mining operations, and furnish plans of attack, he was promptly asked, "In how long a time do you think your army could take my fortress?" In about a quarter of an hour, answered Sturt in his quiet way. "No, no," said the Meer with some indignation, "I am sure you could not do so in so short a time;" and then he paused, evidently making up his mind to tell us a story. After a little, out it came. "That Feringhis should take my fortress, the strongest in the world, in a quarter of an hour is impossible, for it took me, with five hundred horsemen, double that time." Then, apparently forgetting his anger in the anxiety to recount his own exploits, he continued, "when I took possession of this fort I left my army at a little distance, and selecting a few expert warriors, I gallopped up to the gate of the fortress, which I found *open*. I dashed in before the enemy were alarmed, and immediately proclaimed that the place was taken by the victorious Merr Walli. The fools believed me, and all ran away. By-and-bye my army came up and marched quietly in."

We had heard some time before that Dost Mahommed's eldest son, Meer Ufzul Khan, was in Koollum, and it must be confessed that this circumstance did not much contribute to our sense of security, for we could not but feel that we might fairly expect he would not lose so palpable an opportunity of doing us harm should he be so disposed. One morning he sent us a polite message to request an interview, which of course was readily granted. He came, looking pale and sorrowful, and his tone and manner soon satisfied us that his intentions were peaceable. After the usual compliments he entered on the subject of his father's present position and political prospects; he remarked that our *star was too bright*, and assured us that his father was anxious to accede to any terms which the British might think fit to impose short of banishing him to India, and strongly urged us to write to our Government to that effect. We explained to Ufzul Khan that we had received no instructions to act in a political capacity, and that any interference on our part with the affairs of the nation might be looked upon by our superiors as an unwarrantable piece of presumption. He seemed much disappointed at the reply, and, at last, Sturt promised to write and mention the conversation to the authorities, which he did. I am not certain whether he wrote to Dr. Lord or Sir William M'Naghten, nor can be positive that his letter ever reached its destination––at all events, it was of no avail. Ufzul Khān endeavoured to persuade us to remain at Koollum till his father should arrive, who, he said, had escaped from his prison at Bokhara by the assistance of the chief of Shere Subz, as I have already noticed, and was now making his way to the territories of the Meer Walli by a circuitous route, so as to elude the vigilance of the king, and frustrate his endeavours to recapture him. We were much pleased to find that Ufzul Khan had no suspicion of our not being free agents, and Sturt answered he regretted much that the shortness of the time we had yet at our disposal would prevent his complying with his request, which, indeed, considering all the circumstances of the case, it would have been an act of most culpable folly to have acceded to. At the conclusion of this interview Sturt presented him with a handsome rifle, which he received with the utmost gratitude, saying that he was now poor and had nothing to offer in return but his thanks, which, however, he hoped we would believe to be sincere.

No sooner had Meer Ufzul taken his leave than the Meer Walli made his appearance with the evident intention of ascertaining the results of our interview, and the part we were disposed to take in any negociation concerning the Dost. The Meer was apparently anxious to remain on good terms with both parties, or, in other words, preferred having two strings to his bow. "Should the Dost claim my protection," said he, "how would you advise me to act?-- He is your enemy, yet I must not abandon him, or deliver him into the hands of the British; for, although I do not wish to offend the British Government, I owe my present power to the influence of the Ameer,--he has always been my patron, and I must be his friend. And then, moreover, you are the first British officers I have seen since your army took possession of Affghanistān; no notice has been taken of me, the Meer Walli of Koollum; yet, to the petty chiefs of Bameeān vakeels and friendly messages have been sent, with valu- able presents--while, to my repeated letters courting an amicable alliance, not even an answer has been given.--Is it courteous to treat an inferior so?--Is it the conduct generally adopted by the first na- tion in the world? The doubtful way in which your Government has behaved leaves me uncertain as to how my conduct will be inter- preted,--but, if *you* will represent that the Meer Walli wishes to be on terms of amity, I shall consider you as my best friends. Indeed, I would have it known I wish to remain as neutral as possible in any political struggle that may take place."--Here he paused, as if ex- pecting some answer which would be a guide to him, but, receiving none, he at length continued: "I will receive the Dost and be kind to him until he recovers from the fatigues of his journey, and then will beg him to leave Koollum."--It was obvious enough that a consid- eration for himself was the only motive which really influenced our worthy guest, who, it was clear, would gladly have betrayed his former patron if he could have induced us to guarantee an adequate reward to himself. Of course we did not feel authorised to hold out any such prospect, and endeavoured to convince him of the truth that we were not employed in any political capacity, and could not possibly interfere without exposing ourselves to severe animadver- sions from our superiors. I could not but feel the truth of the Meer's remarks on our policy in conciliating the petty chiefs, whilst the friendly overtures of the more powerful were treated almost with insulting neglect.

From the expression of the Meer's sentiments during this inter- view, we concluded that, however great a rascal his highness might eventually prove, still his present policy was to be on good terms with us, and all anxiety on our part as to being forcibly detained was allayed, so that we began now seriously to determine on our future proceedings. As one of the principal objects I had in view on joining Sturt was to procure coins and those relics of antiquity so abundant in the neighbourhood of Balkh, I was most anxious to prosecute my journey hither, and accordingly took an opportunity of explaining to the Meer my wishes and intentions, requesting him to furnish me with an adequate escort for my protection. He evinced a decided unwillingness to facilitate my advance, treating my anxiety to collect coins as an assumed reason to conceal some other more important motive. This was very provoking, but, by this time, we were so much accustomed to have the true and simple account of our plans and intentions treated with civil incredulity, that we felt almost disposed to allow the frequent insinuations of our concealed political character to remain uncontradicted--so useless were all our endeavours to satisfy the natives as to our real position. In vain I urged upon the Meer the emptiness of all his professions of friendship if he now declined to assist me in the manner I clearly pointed out; all was of no avail; on the contrary, the more urgent I became the more obstinate he grew, and I at last was painfully convinced, not only that he disbelieved me, but that he had not the slightest intention of permitting us to proceed across his frontier in the direction of the territories of the King of Bokhārā. He objected that it was a long journey from Cābul to Balkh merely to pick up "rubbish;" and though the actual danger was only for a short space, yet, if any accident happened, if, as he declared was highly probable, we were seized and carried into slavery, he should have to answer to the British Government. His horsemen too would be an insufficient protection against an attack from the numerous hordes of thieves who infested the desert, and would surely be on the alert to pounce upon so valuable a booty. He continued repeating these arguments till we lost all hope of persuading him, and not deeming it advisable to risk a rupture of our present apparently good understanding, we reluctantly submitted and turned our thoughts homewards.[*]

[* Note: The anxiety I have here shewn to procure the escort from the Meer will perhaps appear uncalled for, but those who delight in numismatological specimens will agree with me that the disappointment was not trifling, as only a few travellers had succeeded in obtaining rare coins, and I had every reason to believe other varieties were to be found.]

No sooner was it rumoured in the bazaar that we were about to return to Cabul, than several Hindoo bankers waited upon us to pay their respects and offer whatever sums of money we might require for the journey. They were all very anxious to lend, and were much dissatisfied at the insignificant amount of the cash we required, though the only security was a written promise that we would pay the amount to a certain banker in Cabul on our return; they offered us as much as ten thousand rupees, and appeared very anxious to avail themselves of the opportunity of sending money to Cabul. At all events their confidence was a gratifying proof of the high estimation in which the British name was held in that remote country.

Fac-Simile Drawings of Ancient Coins found in Toorkisthan and Affghanistan,
in the possession of Capt. Burslem.

Description of Coins.

No. A Bactrian coin: legend on the obverse, [Transliterated from the Greek lettering, Basileus ermaion sot]. Reverse, Hercules on a tuckt or throne, with his right arm extended.

No. A square copper coin of Apollodotus: legend,
2. [Transliterated from the Greek lettering, Basileus pollodot soter]; a male figure, holding in one hand a club, and a spear in the other. The reverse bears Pelhvic characters.

No. A square copper coin of Eucratides: [Transliterated from the Greek, Basileus megal] is only decypherable. If of Eucratides the Great, of which I have no doubt, this coin is of great value, as he reigned in Bactria 181 B.C. The reverse bears a Pelhvic legend, with the figures of two warriors mounted.

No. A square silver coin of Menander. A helmeted
4. head, with the inscription, [Transliterated from the Greek, Basileus soteros Menandrou]. The reverse bears the emblematic figure of an owl.

No. A square copper coin, inscription illegible. On
5.   the obverse is a woman holding a flower or a
priest offering incense. It appears to be a Kanirkos coin.

No. A round silver Indo-Scythian coin.
6.

No. A square silver coin of Apollodotus, 195 B.C. Ob-
7.   verse, an elephant, with the Bactrian monogram
beneath––[Transliterated from the Greek, Basileus
pollodoton soteros]. Reverse, an Indian bull. The
characters and figures on this coin are very distinct.

No. Another coin of Menander. An elephant's head
8.   with the proboscis elevated: legend, [Transliterated
from the Greek, Basileus soteros Menandrou]. On
the reverse is a cannon. This is an old and valuable
coin.

No. A gold coin, supposed by Lady Sale to be a Kadphis-
9. es. The legend begins with Amokad and ends with Korano. On the reverse is a naked figure, with the right arm stretched out. A few specimens, but in copper, have been found in the barrow at Maunikya-la in the Punjaub. Lady Sale considers this coin to be a great beauty and of value.

No. A gem found in the plain of Buggram.
10.

CHAPTER XV.

After a most friendly parting interview with the Meer Walli, when he presented us with a horse and baggage pony, we started from Koollum on the 22nd of July, accompanied, by the Meer's special directions, by one of his confidential servants to act ostensibly as our guide, but who, probably, had also his secret instructions to report on all such of our proceedings as might in any way affect the interests of his master.

We proposed to diverge from the route by which we had advanced, at Heibuk, passing through Ghoree, in the territories of the Koondooz chief, and returning to Badjghār by the Dushti Suffaed pass, which Start was very anxious to survey.

Our first day's march brought us to Hazree Sultan, and the next morning we reached Heibuk, where we were cordially welcomed by our old friend Meer Baber Beg, and had again to undergo the infliction of that detestable compound of grease, flour, salt, and tea, which the Meer in his hospitality was always pressing us to swallow.

On our departure the next morning, he sent us a present of a horse; an indifferent one, 'tis true, but, at least, it marked his kindly feeling; he warned us not to delay longer than was absolutely necessary in the country of Meer Moorad Beg, whom he described in no very flattering terms; and he, moreover, cautioned us against the

Koondooz fever, which he declared would inevitably attack us if we were not very careful in selecting our encamping ground at a distance from the pestilential marshes which skirted the bases of the hills. We thanked him for his friendly advice, and started for Rhobāt, where we arrived after a dismal ride of twenty-two miles. The country through which we travelled was perhaps the most dreary portion of Toorkisthān; for about twelve miles we traversed a dry low grass jungle of about a foot in height, tenanted by a species of wild goat, several of which we disturbed on our passage through their haunts, but not being prepared for any sport, I did not take advantage of their unwariness.

The road was utterly devoid of water for a space of full sixteen miles, at the end of which we came upon a scanty supply, scarce sufficient for our immediate necessities and utterly inadequate for a force of any magnitude. The pista tree, the fruit of which is carried to the Indian market, was seen here in considerable quantities; it is very similar in its growth and foliage to the Dauk of Hindoostan.

The *assa fœtida* shrub also abounded on the neighbouring hills, and we were almost overpowered by the horrible stench exhaled therefrom. It is collected in its wild state and sent to Cābul and India, yielding a good profit to those who pick it, as it is used very generally throughout the East for kabobs and curries. We also observed, that day, several coveys of chikore.

At Rhobat is an old caravanserai for travellers, the remains of a very fine and extensive building, with accommodation and apartments all round the square of about twenty-four yards. It is said to have been constructed in the time of the famous Abdoollah Khan, and was reduced to its present desolate state by Meer Moorad Beg, the chief of Koondooz, who some years ago ravaged the whole of this district, burning and laying waste whatever he could not carry off.

On the 25th of July we marched to Ghoree, a distance of about 21 miles. As we approached it, we enjoyed a fine prospect of the extensive savannahs of grass so characteristic of Toorkisthān; many horses were feeding in the distance, and the vale, flanked by low hills, was bounded only by the horizon. We were told that it extended in a right line upwards of thirty miles, and that it was frequently used for horse-racing, the customary length of the course being upwards of twenty miles. We were now in the territories of Meer Moorad Beg, a chief of notorious character, but, trusting to the continuance of the good fortune which had hitherto attended us, we did not make ourselves uncomfortable about him. We could not much admire his town of Ghoree, which, with his fort, was situate on the edge of a morass extending from the limits of the savannah to the foot of the hills--I should think that the fever so prevalent in these districts must be in a great degree attributable to the absolute want of drainage and the decomposition of vegetable matter. Its position was most insalubrious, for the marshy swamps commenced at the very base of hills, and thus as it were encircled the savannahs with a belt of miasma.

The ague, which is usually accompanied by fever, is of a kind very difficult to shake off, gradually weakening the sufferer till he sinks under its influence; the natives themselves are by no means free from its strokes, to which attacks every stranger who remains for many days in the vicinity of the marshes is liable. Though a veil of mystery still covers the particulars of poor Moorcroft's fate, it seems more than probable that he fell a victim to the fever of this country, though the seed that was sown did not mature till some time after he had quitted it.

The fort of Ghoree has great strength, being on a level with the adjacent country and surrounded by a wet ditch thirty feet wide and very deep; its stagnant water teemed with fish of a large size, but I had no opportunity of ascertaining their species. There was a rude drawbridge across the moat, and the dwellings around the fort were temporary hovels composed of straw; so suspicious were the occupants of our intentions that they would not allow us access to the interior of the fort. While reposing at the door of my tent on the evening of our arrival at Ghoree, I was accosted by an old man, with the usual request for a little medicine, as one of his family was afflicted with rheumatism; I gave from our now much reduced medicine chest what I thought at least could do no harm, and endeavoured, as was my custom, to engage the old gentleman in conversation. I have before mentioned the propensity of these people for *story-telling*, and I much fear that when, with their native acuteness in discriminating character, they detect an anxiety on the part of the questioner for old stories, no difficulty exists in the concoction of one for him. In the case now alluded to, I beg to assure my readers that I do not in the slightest degree pledge myself for the veracity of the story which the old man related to me. I should not like even to say that the customs to which he alluded were really *"bonâ fide"* the customs of his country; however, I give it as it was related, nothing doubting that it will be received with due caution, and, at all events, though it may not be received as a legend really characteristic of Toorkisthān weddings, it has indisputable claims to illustrate the habits of Toorkisthān *story-tellers*.

I was remarking to him on the beauty and extent of his savannahs, and, in assenting to what I said, he observed that they were frequently the theatre of wedding races; having soon engaged my attention, he proceeded to narrate the following story, founded perhaps on the numerous outrages of which the despised Huzareh tribe were the victims.

"Far up in one of the numerous valleys of the Yakkoollung country," he commenced, "resided an ancient couple, whose occupation throughout the summer day consisted in storing food for the winter season, and who, when their work was finished, continued mournfully to dwell on the all-absorbing subject of the forcible abduction of their daughter by one of the Uzbeg chiefs.

"Two years and more had now passed since the outrage was perpetrated by a party of Uzbeg horsemen, who, ever bent on plunder and bloodshed, made an incursion into the valley, visiting the different forts at the time when the male inhabitants were employed in the labour of cultivation, and seizing numerous youths and maidens. On the occasion alluded to, among the number of victims was the only daughter of the aged Huzareh peasants, who was considered amongst her tribe as a perfect Peri--'A maid with a face like the moon, scented like musk, a ravisher of hearts, delighting the soul, seducing the senses, and beautiful as the full moon,' She was placed for security behind one of the best mounted of the robbers, whilst the other helpless wretches were driven unresistingly before the horsemen like a flock of sheep, till the abductors reached their own independent territory.

"Before the close of that ill-fated day, the mothers and relations of the stolen were rushing in frantic despair through the fields, announcing to the husbands and fathers the misfortune which had overtaken them.

"The men immediately quitted their work, and armed only with their implements of labour pursued the ravishers for many a mile; but what could they do on foot against so many horsemen? Perhaps it was fortunate for them that they could not overtake the robbers, for they would only have become additional victims. They returned home to bewail their unhappy fate and curse the cruel authors of their misery.

"It happened about a year afterwards that the old man's son returned from Candahār, to enjoy, as he anticipated, a few weeks' happiness with his aged parents and blooming sister; but no sooner had he crossed the threshhold and received the blessing of his trembling parents, than he was made aware of the desolation that had passed over his house. Vowing vengance on the perpetrators of this foul act, and calling down the anger of heaven on all the generation of Uzbegs, the brave Azeem left his home, and abandoning all hopes of repose, busied himself in collecting a band of athletic and desperate young men, who swore on the Korān their determination to have revenge or perish in the attempt. Young Azeem was unanimously chosen commander of the party, and the next morning at break of day, without further preparation beyond taking a small supply of food, they started on their journey. Travelling long days, and resting short nights in the crevices of the mountains, after eighteen days' toil, they at length reached a part of Tartary, distant only two days' march from the fort belonging to the robber Uzbegs who had so cruelly injured them. It now became necessary to advance with more circumspection, as they could no longer depend upon the peasants for protection in the less friendly country they had reached, so separating into several small parties they approached stealthily the Uzbeg fort; some kept the hills on either side, while the rest followed the winding of the grassy plains. Thus proceeding, they formed a kind of circle round the fort, so that they could notice the ingress or departure of its tenants on every side. The fort appeared too strong for an open attack, and when, at night, the leaders of the detached parties assembled to discuss their future plans and to report what they had seen during the day, it was determined to lie in ambush another day for the chance of the main body of the Uzbegs quitting their fort on some foray, so that they would have a better chance, should it become necessary to attack it. Providence seemed to favour their designs, for early next morning considerable parties of Uzbegs were seen issuing from the fort and proceeding towards a large savannah, where some festival was evidently in preparation--for, from the quantity of women and children who accompanied the horsemen, it was clear that fighting was not the business of the day.

"Anxiously did Azeem and his followers watch the movements of their unsuspecting enemy, and soon, from the nature of the preparations going forward, they discovered that a wedding race was about to take place. It was instantly determined to allow the ceremony to proceed, and the capture of the bride was to be the signal for all the Huzarehs to rush in and carry out their object.

"And now the suitors of the maiden, nine in number, appear in the field, all unarmed, but mounted on the best horses they can procure; while the bride herself, on a beautiful Turkoman stallion, surrounded by her relations, anxiously surveys the group of lovers. The conditions of the bridal race were these:--The maiden has a certain start given, which she avails herself of to gain a sufficient distance from the crowd to enable her to manage her steed with freedom, so as to assist in his pursuit the suitor whom she prefers. On a signal from the father all the horsemen gallop after the fair one, and whichever first succeeds in encircling her waist with his arm, no matter whether disagreeable or to her choice, is entitled to claim her as his wife. After the usual delays incident upon such interesting occasions, the maiden quits the circle of her relations, and putting her steed into a hand gallop, darts into the open plain. When satisfied with her position, she turns round to the impatient youths, and stretches out her arms towards them, as if to woo their approach. This is the moment for giving the signal to commence the chace, and each of the impatient youths, dashing his pointed heels into his courser's sides, darts like the unhooded hawk in pursuit of the fugitive dove. The savannah was extensive, full twelve miles long and three in width, and as the horsemen sped across the plain the favoured lover became soon apparent by the efforts of the maiden to avoid all others who might approach her.

"At length, after nearly two hours' racing, the number of pursuers is reduced to four, who are all together, and gradually gaining on the pursued; with them is the favourite, but alas! his horse suddenly fails in his speed, and as she anxiously turns her head she perceives with dismay the hapless position of her lover; each of the more fortunate leaders, eager with anticipated triumph, bending his head on his horse's mane, shouts at the top of his voice, "I come, my Peri; I'm your lover." But she, making a sudden turn, and lashing her horse almost to fury, darts across their path, and makes for that part of the chummun, *plain*, where her lover was vainly endeavouring to goad on his weary steed.

"The three others instantly check their career, but in the hurry to turn back two of the horses are dashed furiously against each other, so that both steeds and riders roll over on the plain. The maiden laughed, for she well knew she could elude the single horseman, and flew to the point where her lover was. But her only pursuer was rarely mounted and not so easily shaken off; making a last and desperate effort he dashed alongside the maiden, and, stretching out his arm, almost won the unwilling prize; but she, bending her head to her horse's neck, eluded his grasp and wheeled off again. Ere the discomfited horseman could again approach her her lover's arm was around her waist, and amidst the shouts of the spectators they turned towards the fort.

"Alas! this was the agreed signal amongst the Huzarehs, who, screened by the undulations of the savannah or hidden in the watercourses, had been anxiously awaiting the event. With a simultaneous shout they rush in upon the unprepared multitude, and commence an indiscriminate massacre; but short was their success, for a distant party of Uzbegs were observed rapidly gallopping to the scene of action, and the Huzarehs were compelled to retire, their spirit for vengeance yet unslaked. The panic their sudden onslaught had caused was so great that they might all have retired unmolested had not Azeem suddenly recognized his sister amongst a group of females who were being hurried towards the fort. Regardless of the almost certain death that awaited him he rushed to embrace her, but hardly had he clasped her in his arms when the chief of the harem drove his Persian dagger through his back. At sight of this all thoughts of further revenge were abandoned, and the Huzarehs hastily quitting the field made the best of their way home, not without having, though at the expense of the life of their leader, inflicted a severe punishment on the invaders of their peaceful country,"[*]

[* Note: Clark, in his Travels in Russia and Tartary, describes the ceremony of marriage among the Calmucks as performed on horseback.

> "The girl is first mounted and rides off at full
> speed. Her lover pursues, and if he overtakes her
> she becomes his wife, and the marriage is con-
> summated on the spot; after which she returns
> with him to his tent. But it sometimes happens that
> the woman does not wish to marry the person by
> whom she is pursued, in which case she will not
> suffer him to overtake her; and we were assured
> that no instance occurs of a Calmuck girl being
> caught, unless she has a partiality for her pursuer.
> If she dislikes him she rides, to use the language of
> an English sportsman, 'neck or nothing,' until she
> has completely escaped, or until the pursuer's
> horse is tired out, leaving her at liberty to return,
> and to be afterwards chased by some more favour-
> ite admirer."]

Such was the old man's tale; whether the offspring of his fertile imagination, or actually founded upon fact, so plausible did it appear, and so much interested was I in his narration, that it became forcibly imprinted on my memory, and I have minutely followed him in its details.

The morning after our arrival at Ghoree several of our followers were taken ill, and as all were in great dread of the Koondooz fever, a considerable alarm prevailed in our small camp. We did not at first think much of the sickness, which we attributed to too free an indulgence in the Koondooz melon, which is of a very large size, and equal in flavour to those of Cabul. We therefore determined to remain a day or two at Ghoree, in the hopes of a favourable change taking place. But on the third day it was evident that the Koondooz fever had really made its appearance, and several of the guard and servants, to the number of twenty and upwards, were so much weakened as to be unable to proceed. In this dilemma we deemed it advisable not to remain any longer in the vicinity of the marshes, and resolved to proceed with such of our men as were still healthy, to survey the Dushti Suffaed Pass, already alluded to. We determined on leaving the sick and the greater portion of our baggage behind, and despatched a letter to Meer Moorad Beg, requesting permission for them to remain at Ghoree till our return, which we hoped would not be delayed beyond a few days. The ruler of Koondooz civilly acceded to our request, and sent us many friendly messages, but hardly sufficient to dispel our uneasiness at leaving even for so short a time such temptation for the gratification of his predatory propensities; but we had the choice of two evils––our time was so short that if we all remained together at Ghoree, not only might the ravages of the fever become more serious, but the opportunity would be lost of examining the pass. Before leaving Ghoree we received a message from the governor of the fort, apologizing for his inability to visit us, with the excuse that there being much treachery and ill will in the neighbourhood, he dare not quit his post, lest he fall under the dreaded displeasure of Meer Moorad Beg.

We now dismissed, with a dress of honour and letter of thanks, the *confidential* man whom the Meer Walli of Koollum had ordered to accompany us, and leaving the greater part of our medicine chest for the use of the sick, we started on the 28th of August. Before our departure we received a further proof of the friendly disposition of Moorad Beg, in the shape of a beautiful Toorkmān saddle, not larger than an English racing one; the flaps were richly embroidered, and the steel pommel was inlaid with inscription in gold of sentences from the Korān.

CHAPTER XVI.

We were now about to explore a part of Toorkisthān which I have reason to believe had never been visited by Europeans; the distance between Ghoree and Badjgh[=]ar is about eighty miles, across as wild and romantic a country as can well be conceived, consisting of a succession of difficult and in some places perilous defiles; the last of these was the famous Dushti Suffaed, which leads to Badjghār. There is a sameness in the features of these Toorkisthān passes which renders a faithful description tedious, from its monotony and the necessary repetition of similar characteristic features; yet the reader will hardly fail to draw important conclusions from the immense difficulty and almost practical impossibility that a modern army of considerable numbers, with all its incumbrances, through such a country, with any hope of its retaining its efficiency or even a tithe of its original numerical strength, will encounter. And when we consider that the passes of Toorkisthān embrace only a small part of the distance to be traversed by an army from the west, we may well dismiss from our minds that ridiculous impression, once so unfortunately prevalent in India, that is now justly denominated *Russophobia.* What a fearful amount of human suffering might have been averted! what national disgrace might have been avoided! and what millions of treasure saved, had the authorities in India but examined the practicability of an invasion which Russia had too much wisdom ever seriously to contemplate!

But to return to our wanderings. As I said before, we left Ghoree early in the morning of the 28th, and soon reached the foot of the hills, ascending a narrow valley which gradually contracted into a rocky ravine. As we traversed the higher levels all vegetation ceased, excepting the Pista tree already alluded to; yet there must have been some herbage in the gullies, as we saw several flocks of wild goats, so wild indeed that it was impossible to get within rifle range of them. We had heard of a place called Shullāctoo, within the distance of a day's march, and conceiving naturally that it was a habitation of men, we determined to pass the night there. As the evening advanced, the aspect of the country assumed a still wilder and more desolate character, our cattle began to show symptoms of distress, and as the hills were apparently destitute of water, we became a little uneasy regarding the nature of our billet. A sudden turn of the ravine brought us to a small open space, without a blade of grass or a vestige of any thing human, which our guide complacently informed us was Shullāctoo, a mere "locus standi." After the first feeling of dismay had subsided, we recollected that we had a small supply of food for our horses; and water being now found for the first time since we entered the hills,--and we had come a good sixteen miles,--we determined not to proceed further, so pitching our little tent we made ourselves as comfortable as circumstances would admit.

On the 29th we marched, a distance of fourteen miles, to a small fort called Keune. But I unfortunately commenced the day's work by losing my way amongst the rocks, with some of the guard: after wandering for some hours, surrounded by scenery the grandeur of which I should better have appreciated under different circumstances, one of the Affghān soldiers hit upon a pathway, and seeing a man in the distance, he made for, and, seizing him in the most unceremonious manner, brought him to me. The poor fellow was in the greatest state of alarm; he had evidently never seen a Feringhi before, and fancied that his last hour had arrived. I put a rupee into his hand, and endeavoured to make him understand that we were neither robbers nor murderers, but travellers who had lost their way; he was naturally incredulous, for certainly our appearance gave but small indication of our respectable character.[*] At length we were obliged to intimate that his fears might be realized unless he showed us the way to Keune, which we eventually reached in the evening, much exhausted with our excursion.

[* Note: I was armed with a huge old-fashioned sword of the 11th dragoons, purchased in the Cabul bazaar, (marked D-XI Dr.) and clad in a green Swiss frock. I had a coloured turban wound in copious folds round my head as a protection from the sun, beard of nearly three months' growth, and accompanied by a ferocious-looking tribe of Affghans, all unshorn as well as myself, created anything but a prepossessing impression to a stranger. The reader will not, therefore, feel surprised at the man's hesitation in meeting us.]

The chief of the fort at first declined furnishing us with any supplies, though we offered liberal payment, declaring that he had only sufficient for his own consumption; he, however, relented, and sent us enough for our immediate wants. He afterwards came himself, and informed us that we had acted very unwisely in mentioning at Ghoree the route we proposed to follow, as one of the Sheikkallee Huzareh chiefs, who was in a state of rebellion, had passed through Keune the day before, and had stated that a party of Feringhis were about to pass through his country with a quantity of odd looking boxes filled with money, (alluding, I suppose, to the theodolite, &c.) and that he would with his whole tribe waylay and rob us. This was pleasant news, but we took the hint and determined to be on our guard. In return for this piece of information, the inhabitants of Keune expressed a desire to see the *Feringhis feed*; rather a novel request, but one which we easily gratified by striking the walls of the tent while we eat our dinner. The natives squatted down in a circle outside the tent pins, and watched every morsel we put into our mouths with the utmost interest and with many exclamations of surprise and astonishment; and when before retiring for the night we as usual had a skinful of water poured over us, their wonder knew no bounds; they were evidently but slightly acquainted with the use of water as applied for the purposes of cleanliness.

We left Keune at daybreak on the 30th, hoping to be able to make our way to Badjghār, distant about forty-five miles, by surmounting the Keune pass and proceeding down the Surruk Kulla valley. The ascent was long and steep, the distance we had to travel before reaching the summit being above thirteen miles; and though we had been on the move nearly all day, such were the difficulties of the pass that night overtook us shortly after we had reached its crest.

Not a sign of habitations or trace of cultivation was visible; we had no corn for our cattle, but fortunately the more sheltered spots in the vicinity of water were clothed with luxuriant grass, which the horses greedily eat. Our followers had, with the improvidence of Asiatics, brought but a scanty supply of food, and indeed we were all to blame for having trusted too much to the wild mountains for supplies. There were plenty of chikore, however, and as I had succeeded in shooting two or three in the morning we were not entirely without food; and having pitched our tent, we retired to rest in the hope that the next day we should come upon some fort where we might recruit.

As we were preparing to start early on the morning of the 31st, we met a traveller pursuing his solitary way to Keune, who, after expressing his wonder at encountering a party of Feringhis in such a place, inquired our proposed route. We informed him that our intention was to proceed over the Surruk Kulla pass and make our way to Badjghar, but he cautioned us not to attempt any such thing; for though the road was better than the more direct one, called the Espion Pass, it was infested by a robber tribe from whose hands he had himself only escaped, not having any thing to lose.

This unwelcome intelligence induced Sturt to change his plan, and we agreed that having done our utmost to fulfil the wishes of government in ascertaining the nature of the passes in the vicinity of Badjghar, it was our duty to consult the safety of ourselves and followers, and get them as soon as possible within reach of protection. We had no food of any kind left, but after all we did not anticipate much serious evil from a forced fast of forty-eight hours; so, after rewarding our wanderer for his very seasonable warning, we struck off to cross the Espion Pass. The event proved how imminent had been our danger, for after reaching Badjghar we were made aware that a large body of horsemen had assembled in the Surruk Kullah valley for the purpose of attacking us––that they had come up the road to meet us, and had actually reached the point where we turned off about two hours after us.

We travelled the whole of the 31st August across a succession of broken passes; so complicated were the valleys and so broken were the range of hills, that we were unable to tell when we reached the back-bone of the ridge, and we struggled on in doubt and difficulty till we were again overtaken by the shades of night.

Our cattle were quite exhausted; our followers grumbling, dispirited, and frightened, the prospect of a second bivouac by no means improving their discipline and insubordination.

While I was endeavouring to pacify them by the only argument I had at my disposal, founded on the principle of "*levius fit patientiâ quidquid corrigere est nefas,*" one of our servants brought us the joyful news that from an eminence adjacent he had discovered an abatta, or clump of blanket tents, surrounded by cultivated land, about a mile off. Where tents were, food would probably be obtainable; and as we were not in a condition to be very particular as to the character of the inhabitants, we immediately despatched an embassy with money to purchase whatever edible substances they could procure. Our anxieties were now relieved by the return of our mission, driving before them a couple of very thin sheep, and carrying a small supply of corn for the cattle. With this reasonable supply we made a tolerable meal, and succeeded in putting the discontented into a better frame of mind.

We determined to make a push next morning for Badjghar, and started before day-break for the Dushti Suffäed Pass, the crest of which we reached after travelling a distance of about nine miles over very bad ground. We were now *"en pays de connoissance,"* but our cattle were so much weakened by the work and privations of the last three or four days, that we could not attempt the long and difficult descent into the valley beneath. I therefore rode on alone and reached Badjghar in a few hours. I immediately visited Capt. Hay, and having procured a supply of food, returned with it the same night to the party, much exhausted with my trip, but satisfied now that there could be no further cause for grumbling on the part of our followers.

The state of our baggage-equipage next morning was so bad, that Sturt thought it advisable to give them another day's rest, and he went on himself to Badjghar; but in the course of the day I received an express from him, stating that circumstances had occurred which made it absolutely necessary for me to bring in the whole party without delay. I knew Sturt too well to doubt the urgency he represented, and in spite of lame legs, sore backs, &c. I managed to bring all hands safe into Badjghar late on the evening of the 2d of August. Our men were taken every care of, (which indeed they required, as fever and ague had weakened them much,) and in a few days all traces of their sufferings had disappeared; but poor Sturt, who had been complaining for some days before of great debility and headache, was seized on the morning of the 3d with a violent attack of Koondooz fever, which soon prostrated his strength and caused me some uneasiness. He weathered the storm, however, and by the 11th was sufficiently recovered to enable him to resume his duties.

I have before mentioned, I think, that we had left some of our followers and a considerable portion of our baggage at Ghoree, intending to return to that fort after visiting the passes which I have alluded to; but on our reaching Badjghar we found that the clouds which had been gathering for some time past in the political horizon had assumed so threatening an appearance that it would be madness to attempt to prosecute our examination of the nature of the country, when its wild and lawless population were in such an excited state. The intentions of the Koondooz ruler were not known, and we felt very anxious for the safety of the sick whom we had been necessitated to leave at Ghoree, as in addition to his natural sympathy for a fellow-creature's sufferings, Sturt feared that if any misfortune befel them, he might, though unjustly, be accused of having deserted them. His uneasiness was increased by receipt of a letter from Ghoree from one of our people, in which it was stated that the baggage we had left behind had been opened and some things abstracted, and that they themselves were in imminent danger of being seized and sold as slaves.

After making every allowance for the exaggerations of fear, there was still sufficient in this communication to aggravate poor Start's difficulties; he was in doubt whether to assume a high tone, or to endeavour by flattery to save his followers, and his last act before the violence of the fever obliged him to succumb was a firm but respectful letter which he wrote to Meer Moorād Beg, in which he stated that reports inconsistent with that chief's known good faith had reached him; that he had heard that his property had been seized and his people threatened; that he was sure they were lies invented by Moorād Beg's enemies to create a bad feeling towards him; and that he requested the men and property might be immediately forwarded safe to Cabul. Those who are familiar with the vanity and punctiliousness on points of etiquette of the chieftains of the Hindoo Khoosh will easily conceive how much depended upon the wording of this letter.

In the written intercourse between equals it is customary to put the impression of the signet at the top of the sheet, but from an inferior such an act would be considered as highly presumptuous. Sturt, though advised to assume the humble tone, was resolute in putting his seal at the beginning of the letter, and the event proved that his judgment was as usual correct, for though (it was stated) the chief of Koondooz was but a few months after in arms against the British, yet our people and property were safely forwarded to us at Cabul.

CHAPTER XVII.

It was only after my arrival at Badjghar with the men that I became acquainted with Sturt's reasons for requesting me to come in without delay, Capt Hay was in daily expectation of the arrival of a convoy from Bameeān with a supply of provisions, clothing, and ammunition for the use of his regiment, and having received information from one of the numerous spies, who gain a livelihood by supplying information to *both* parties, that large bodies of men were assembling in the Kammurd valley, through which the convoy would have to pass, determined, though he did not attach much credit to his informant, to despatch as strong a body as he could spare to reinforce the escort. He accordingly sent out two companies of the Goorkha regiment with directions to proceed to the "Dundun Shikkun Kotul," there to meet the convoy and protect them in their passage through the Kammurd valley. Such was the scarcity of European officers, that Capt. Hay was obliged to intrust the command of the force to the quarter-master-serjeant of his corps; who, though unused to the management of so considerable a party in the field, and who might have been excused if in the hour of need his brain had not been as fertile of expedients as is generally necessary in encounters of this kind, acquitted himself in a manner that would have done credit to the best light infantry officer in the service. I much regret that I cannot record his name, but before being appointed to the Goorkha corps he was a non-commissioned officer in the Bengal European regiment. He was one of the many victims, I fear, of the year 1841, as I have been unable to trace his career. Hundreds of brave European non-commissioned officers met a similar fate, and are merely noticed as having perished in the retreat from Cabul. The many acts of coldblooded treachery which disgraced the Affghans, and which ought to have opened the eyes of those in power to the absurdity in trusting to their faith, were merged in the wholesale murders of Khoord Cabul, Jugdulluk, and Gundummuk.

I have before described the narrowness of the valley up to Kammurd and the lofty ranges of precipitous hills by which it is flanked; and the reader will perhaps recollect my noticing two forts on either side of the river a little above Piedbāgh. It was here that the Serjeant halted his party after the first day's march, intending to proceed the next morning to the Dundun Shikkun pass to meet the convoy. At day-light he was informed that the expected convoy had not crossed the pass, and while forming his men to proceed and ascertain whether the report was correct or otherwise, he was suddenly attacked by large bodies of horse and foot: the serjeant immediately took advantage of the ground to protect his party from the heavy fire which was poured in from all sides, and having observed that the enemy, whoever they were, were in too great a force to leave him a chance of successfully maintaining his position, which was commanded from several points, he determined on retreating to Badjghar, a distance of about nine miles. The valley was full of orchards divided by low walls, and perhaps to a well-disciplined company of steady old soldiers with plenty of officers, a retreat, even in the face of several hundred Uzbegs, might have been effected without loss, by forming the whole body into two lines of skirmishers, and retiring alternately; but the serjeant knew too well the temper of his gallant little mountaineers, who are more famous for bravery than judgment, to trust the safety of his party to the success of a manoeuvre, the chief point in which was to know when to retreat. His first line of skirmishers would never have retired in order, taking advantage of every natural obstacle of the ground for concealment, but would have boldly confronted the cavalry and probably been destroyed to a man. He therefore moved his Goorkhas in quarter distance column steadily along the road, which luckily hugged the precipitous hills on one side, so that the enemy could only avail themselves of the valley on the other side of the road to attack him, the mountains being so impracticable that while they attempted to climb them to turn his flank he had already gained so much ground as to be out of reach of even a "plunging" fire. In ordinary quick time did this little band retire under a heavy though straggling fire from a force many times more numerous than themselves. The serjeant was enabled with difficulty to carry out his plan, which was, not to return the enemy's fire, but to proceed steadily on till he could suddenly take advantage of some protecting ledge of rock or orchard wall behind which he could form his men and confuse the enemy by pouring in a few volleys. He would then form quarter distance columns of subdivisions again, and proceed in his retreat as before. He had no misgivings as to the courage and firmness of his men, for the Goorkhas have ever been noted for their dashing bravery, and an incident soon proved how wisely he had judged in not extending his men. While retiring, a chance shot killed a man who happened to be a great favourite; his nearest comrades immediately halted and faced about, and notwithstanding the commands and entreaties of the serjeant; they determined to avenge his death. Grouping themselves round the body of their dead companion, they awaited the enemy, and when sure that every shot would tell, each man delivered his fire, and then drawing his knife with a yell of defiance, rushed upon hundreds of their foes; to have supported them would have been to lead the whole party to inevitable slaughter, and the authority of the quarter-master-serjeant was scarce sufficient to restrain his men from breaking from their cover to join the unequal fight: as it was, the gallant little band were soon outnumbered, and after a reckless and desperate resistance were literally hacked to pieces. The enemy encouraged by this success now pressed hard upon the Goorkhas, and had they been fortunate enough in getting round to the front not a man would have escaped; as it was, the men were falling very fast, when a happy occurrence changed the aspect of affairs. It seems that a chief, conspicuous from his glittering armour and steel head-piece, mounted on a powerful horse with an armed footman behind him, attracted the notice of the Goorkhas by the cool manner in which he rode up to within a distance of about eighty yards, delivered his fire, then galloped away out of gunshot to allow the gentleman "en croupe" to reload. A few of the men having observed this manoeuvre repeated three or four times, concealed themselves behind a rock, while the main body retired. On came the chief to within his prescribed distance; a volley from behind the rock scarce ten paces off rolled horse and man over and over. The effect on the enemy was such that they kept at a more respectful distance, and after a few random shots discontinued the pursuit. Such was the account the serjeant himself gave me of the fight, and I have no reason to suspect him of exaggeration. He accomplished his arduous retreat with a loss of nineteen men killed, but more than half this number voluntarily sacrificed themselves to avenge the death of their comrade. It is difficult, when relating the numerous acts of heroism of the Goorkha troops, to refrain from drawing invidious comparisons between their conduct and that of the Hindoo soldier during the retreat from Cabul; but though it must be allowed that the despondency and mental enervation which sometimes spreads like an epidemic among Sepoy troops, must importantly deteriorate from their general character as soldiers, still it must be recollected that the physical constitution of the Hindoo incapacitates him from action under some circumstances. Severe cold benumbs his faculties of mind as well as body, and the nature of his ordinary food is such that unless the supply is regular and sufficient his strength fails him; and again, his belief in predestination is strong, and often a trivial reverse will induce him to abandon himself to his fate. But in these days the Hindoo soldier need not fear that his noble and gallant qualities will not be understood or appreciated. Every good soldier will honor the Hindoo for his patient endurance, his courage, and fidelity.

To turn to the convoy: the attempt was made to get the camels laden with ammunition, stores, and provisions over the Dundun Shikkun Pass; but the difficulties were found to be so great that the escort and convoy returned to Syghān, and crossing the Nulli Fursh Kotul, reached their destination.

This was the first glaring instance of the state of the country, and some people may well be astonished it was viewed by the political authorities in so insignificant a light. But I will not too much impose upon the patience of the reader by detailing the execrable reasons which were put forth for the most absurd measures during the twelve months preceding the annihilation of our army.

It was now evident to those who were not obstinately blind that a general rising was contemplated; and a few days after our arrival at Badjghar we heard that Dost Mahommed had arrived at Koollum, and that after all his diplomacy our old friend the Meer Walli had received him with open arms, and was now on his way to attack our out-posts. The authorities were shortly afterwards aroused from their apathy, the advanced troops were very properly withdrawn, the gallant Col. Dennie was sent in command of a small but efficient force to the head of the Bameeān valley, where, as has been before detailed, he repulsed the combined forces of Dost Mahommed Khan, the Meer Walli of Koollum, and all the Uzbeg chiefs.

CHAPTER XVIII.

On the 12th of August we departed from Badjghar on our return to Cābul, and I reached Bameeān by a forced march in two days, preceding Sturt, who was still very weak and obliged to travel more leisurely. I was very nearly suffering from my anxiety to get on, for one of the laden Yabboos, being urged beyond what he considered his lawful rate of progress, lashed out most furiously with both hind legs; luckily, the flap of my saddle received the full force of one of his heels, and the soft part of my leg the other, which lamed me severely for a time.

On the 22nd, Sturt having arrived, we made up our party to visit the ruins of the Castle of Zohawk, distant about ten miles from Bameeān. I was rewarded for my trouble, both from the picturesque nature of the ruins themselves, and because I was fortunate enough again to fall in with one of those professional story-tellers from whom I have already largely quoted. I have indeed listened to many more stories than I have ventured here to insert; some I have reject-ed from the nature of their details, others from there being a strong impression on my mind that they were the extempore invention of the story-teller with a view to the rupee, which he feared he would not secure if he confessed he had nothing to relate. I have not per-haps been judicious in my selection of those which I hoped would amuse the reader, but I have done my best to choose for insertion those which differed the most from each other; and I may be al-lowed to add as an excuse for my apparent credulity regarding the tales themselves, that they are implicitly believed by the inhabitants, so that, making allowance for the corruption of tradition, the facts on which they are founded in all probability did really occur.

The ruins of the Castle of Zohawk are situated on a hill commanding the high road from Toorkisthan over the Irāk and Kalloo passes, and in the angle formed by the union of the Bameeān and Irāk rivers. It is impossible to fix the date of the first structure; it seems from the ruin to have been added to at many successive epochs. The size of the towers appeared very insignificant compared with the extent of ground which the building at one time evidently covered, but perhaps the towers, though small, were numerous. The only one now standing was situated high up the hill, from which a covered passage partly cut through the solid rock leads down to the water side. We had some trouble in gaining the highest point of the ruins, as we were obliged to scramble up the steep face of the precipice, still covered with the remains of walls and bastions, which had been built up wherever the ground was sufficiently level for a foundation. Many dreary-looking cells attracted our notice amongst the ruins, and all the information I could get was, that they were the abode of evil spirits. My informant would, I do believe, have amused me for hours with legends of the said spirits, and indeed every river and lake, every mountain and valley in this district bears its peculiar legend, always improbable, generally absurd, and though from that very cause diverting for the moment, I fear that the naïve taste amongst our "savans" which delighted in the history of Jack the Giant-killer being fast on the wane, they would not be gratified by a lengthy recital; but I must still take the liberty of repeating as well as I could follow the vile jargon of my narrator, a tale which he told me of the Castle of Zohawk while standing on its ruins. He had evidently been accustomed to tell the same story to others, or else I imagine that, in consideration of our both being on the spot, he would have spared a description of what I saw before my eyes. I give it to the reader as nearly as I can in the narrator's words.

"At the extreme end of a precipitous hill jutting out from the main range of mountains at the junction of the Bameeān and Irāk rivers, are the remains of an old castle called Zohawk, after a noted freebooter, who, secure in the strength of his fortress, was the terror of the surrounding villages, and lived by rapine, pillage, and plunder of every kind. To a careless observer the diminutive tower, which alone remains standing, would not convey an adequate idea of the original extent of the castle; but on a close examination the whole face of the mountain will be found to be covered with ruined walls and roofless chambers, now the fit abodes of devils of all sorts and denominations. Many hundreds of years ago, before the invasion of Nadir Shah, Zohawk Khan occupied the castle; he did not build it, but as it acquired an infamous notoriety during his life-time, and has not been inhabited since, it still bears the name of the ferocious robber, who with a band as vicious as himself lived there for many years. Zohawk Khan was originally an Huzareh peasant; he was seized while a child and carried off in slavery to Toorkisthān, where his naturally cruel and savage disposition was exasperated by ill-treatment and fostered by the scenes of wickedness with which he was made familiar. Being very cunning, he soon acquired influence amongst his fellow slaves, and organized a conspiracy, in the fulfilment of which his own master and many other Toorkomaun chiefs were put to death under every refinement of torture. Zohawk at the head of the rebel slaves then traversed the country, robbing the harmless peasants, till he reached the vicinity of the castle, which still bears his name. It was then inhabited by an old Huzareh chieftain, who had formerly been a kind master to Zohawk's parents. Regardless of the memory of past kindness, the ruffian determined to possess himself of this place, and under the pretence of craving the hospitality of the rightful owner, introduced himself and fellow villains into the fortification. In the dead of the night, according to a preconcerted plan, the robbers rose from their place of rest, and stealing to the sleeping apartment of the chieftain, murdered him; the affrighted garrison craved for life, but one after another were placed in irons to be disposed of as slaves. The freebooter, now master of the fortress, assumed the title of Khān, and commenced that career of ruthless cruelty and depravity which more than any thing else causes his name to be remembered and his memory cursed by the present inhabitants of the neighbourhood. The government of the self-styled Khān was a reign of terror, and many were the nameless atrocities committed within the walls of the castle. He had, however, one confidant, whom he believed faithful, but who from interested motives submitted to the savage passions of his master, and being the chief eunuch of the harem, had great influence in that department. It was the custom of Zohawk Khān to choose the autumn of the year for the season of his predatory excursions, and it happened that, while absent with the flower of his force on one of these death-dealing expeditions, a conspiracy was set on foot, the principal agitator being the eunuch of the seraglio. "It was determined that on the evening when the chieftain was expected to return, a general feast should be given to those remaining at home, with the double view of rendering the men who had not joined in the conspiracy incapable from the effects of debauchery in siding with Zohawk, and of exasperating the ferocious chieftain, who was known to be averse to any revelry during his absence. The favourite wife summoned all the harem to a feast, whilst a copious allowance of intoxicating liquor was served out to the minor portion of the garrison. The wine soon produced the required effect, and in the midst of the revelry and uproar the Khān appeared at his castle gate, and without enquiring the cause of the tumult, instantly proceeded to the harem, and lifting the Purdah stood in the presence of his wives. 'What is this?' said he, glancing savagely round.-- 'We expected your return and have prepared a feast to welcome you,' was the ironical reply of the favourite wife, who at the same time trembling in her limbs scarce dared to face the enraged tyrant, 'It is a lie, offspring of a Kaffir; you shall pay the penalty of your disobedience of my orders. Here, Saleh, take her and throw her over the battlements into the river;' but ere the reluctant eunuch could enforce the cruel mandate, the woman raised her hand, and with a small dagger pierced herself to the heart. Unmoved by her tragic fate, Zohawk instantly commanded that four of the other women should be dealt with in the same way, and seeing the eunuch hesitate, drew his Persian blade and rushed at him; but ere the sword fell, the knife of Saleh was sheathed in the ruffian's breast. "The news of his death spread rapidly through the castle; then followed the strife of war. The Khān's party, though in number nearly double that of Saleh, were wearied with their recent foray, and after a desperate conflict of three hours they were driven into one of the wings of the castle, and butchered to a man. Blood flowed in almost every apartment; broken swords, daggers, and matchlocks lay in all directions, shewing how terrible the strife had been. And now, when Zohawk's party had been exterminated, a murmuring arose amongst the victors as to who should be the chief, and Saleh, perceiving that he should gain nothing for the exertions he had made, demanded permission to leave the castle, taking with him as his sole share of booty his sister, who was an inmate of the harem. His terms were immediately complied with, and the wary eunuch lost no time in quitting the scene of blood.

"Those remaining agreed to defer the election of a chief till they had refreshed themselves after their labours: in the heat of intoxication blood again flowed, and after passing the whole night in drinking and fighting, morning appeared to eighteen survivors of the fray. Each still claimed for himself the chieftainship, and while still wrangling on the subject, one of the wounded partizans of Saleh, unperceived by the drunkards, secreted a large bag of powder in the room, and igniting it by a train with his slow match crawled out of the castle.

"The explosion was terrific; down toppled tower and bastion, enveloping in their ruins the remainder of the garrison, and the castle was in a few moments reduced to the shapeless mass which it now presents.

"The wounded author of the catastrophe alone escaped; but the knowledge of his crimes prevented him from returning to his country, and he wandered for many years about the blackened walls, the terror of the neighbourhood, who considered him an evil spirit. He subsisted on herbs growing on the adjacent mountains, till at last he disappeared no one knew where. Since that period, the fortress has never been the resting place of the traveller or the haunt of the freebooter."

Such was the terrible tale of blood and wounds which my informant communicated to me, and certainly, if it rests its foundation on any one of the horrors with which it is filled, the castle of Zohawk does well deserve its bad repute.

On the 23rd we left Bameeān and proceeded over the Irāk pass to Oorgundee, where we arrived on the 28th. No event occurred nor any thing worth mentioning, unless it be the "naïveté" of an old man, who, observing me light my cigar with a lucifer-match, asked in a grave and solemn tone, whether that was indeed fire. I took his finger, and placed it in the flame, much to his astonishment, but convincing him of its reality. He then enquired if it was the fire from heaven, which he heard the Feringhis were possessed of. I endeavoured, but I fear without success, to explain to the old gentleman the nature of fulminating substances, and though he listened with patience, he was evidently still in the dark, when I presented him with the contents of my match-box and shewed him how to ignite them; his gratitude was manifest, as he walked off highly pleased with his toy, which I hope may not have burned his fingers.

Sturt left me on the 29th, being anxious to get back to Cabul; but as I had three days to spare, and my taste for wandering was still unabated, I joined Capt. Westmacott, of the 37th Native Infantry, in a flying excursion into the valley of Charrikār, which the Affghāns consider as the garden of Cabul. The first day we rode from Oorgundee to Shukkur Durra, or "the sugar valley," so called, not from growing that useful article of grocery, but from its fertile orchards and extensive vineyards. After a few miles' ride we crossed a low range of hills, and came upon the flourishing district of Betout,--literally, "without mulberries." The sagacious reader will justly infer that mulberry trees were in profusion every where else; indeed so plentiful are they in general that many of the natives live almost exclusively in winter upon the fruit, which is dried and reduced to a powder, and after being mixed with a little milk, or even water, forms a palatable and nutritious food. The view from the crest of the low range of hills was really enchanting, and strongly contrasted with the wild and craggy mountains amongst which we had of late been struggling. An extensive plain, bounded by high mountains, and again crowned by the snowy peaks of those more distant, lay before us, its whole surface dotted with a multitude of white forts surrounded by a belt of the most vivid green, the barrenness of the uncultivated spots acting as a foil to the rich vegetation which springs under the foot of the Affghān husbandman wherever he can introduce the fertilizing stream. We rode leisurely on through this wilderness of gardens, till on approaching the village of Be-tout the loud wail of women hired to pour forth their lamentations for some misfortune assailed our ears, and on enquiring we learnt that one of the inhabitants had been murdered the preceding night under the following circumstances.

It appears that ten years ago the murdered man (who was a Persian) had a very pretty daughter, and that a neighbouring chief hearing of her beauty caused her to be forcibly seized and conveyed to his own fort. The father, regardless of any consideration but revenge, arming himself with his long Affghān knife, gained admission into the chief's house and immediately cut him down and made his escape. For ten years he concealed himself from the vengeance of the relatives of the chief, but a few days before he had returned to his native village, hoping that time would have softened the vindictiveness of his enemy; but he shewed his ignorance of the Affghān character, with whom revenge is a sacred virtue. He had not been long returned, when a nephew of the chief he had slain shot him through the heart from behind a wall. As we passed through the village we saw the inhabitants crowding round the still unburied corpse of the injured father, and our thoughts were painfully diverted from a contemplation of the richness and plenty which Providence had vouchsafed to this fertile spot, to a mournful consideration of the wild passions of man, who pollutes the earth with the blood of his fellow-creature.

As we proceeded onwards we came upon those luxuriant vineyards which produce the famous Kohistān grape, of enormous size as to berry and bunch, but excelling in delicacy of flavour, in juiciness, and thinness of skin even the far-famed Muscadel.

The vines are trained either upon a trellice work or along the ground, the latter mode being used for the most delicate grape; but it requires more care and attention, it being necessary while the fruit is ripening so to trim the plant and thin its foliage, that the branch may have sufficient sun, and be kept as near as possible to the earth without touching it. This mode of training is adopted in the cultivation of the enormous black grape, called from its size and colour "the cow's-eye." Towards evening we reached the vicinity of Shukkur Durrah, lying at the extremity of the plain and backed by mountains of considerable height. Here we encamped for the night under the shelter of a magnificent walnut tree, in a small garden adjoining the fort.

After we had pitched our tents, many Hindoos who trade in fruit, the staple produce of the country, came to pay their respects, and one of them informed me that about four miles across the mountains to the north-west in the Sheikkallee Huzareh country, there were three lakes so extensive that it occupied a well-mounted horseman a whole day to ride round them. No European, he said, had ever visited them; one gentleman, whose name he did not know, had tried to reach them, but drank so much brandy by the way that he was obliged to lie down instead, and the guide had great difficulty in getting him back. I regretted that the expiration of my leave prevented me from exploring these lakes, which I do not think have ever been examined by any of our engineers; but I hope that, had I undertaken the excursion, I should not have fallen into the same scrape the above mentioned gentleman did. The gardens belonging to the chief were well worth looking at, with a beautiful stream of water flowing through the centre, tortured by artificial rocks into fifty diminutive cataracts.

We were well satisfied with our quarters, but after night-fall intimation was given us that unless we kept a sharp look-out it was very probable we might have some unwelcome intruders before morning, as a neighbouring fort was hostile to that of Shukkur Durrah; and moreover, that the inhabitants of the fort itself were in the utmost dread of a band of desperadoes who infested the adjacent hills and occasionally paid them a nocturnal visit. Luckily for us they were in hourly expectation of such an intrusion, for their fears kept them on the alert, and they had a watchman on each of the towers, whose sonorous voices proclaimed every hour of the night. Our guard was now reduced to six, the remainder being employed to escort Sturt's instruments into Cabul, so that I really did not much like the appearance of things; when about midnight my servant reported to me that the sentry saw a great many lights moving about us.

I instantly rose and distinctly observed the lighted slow matches of firearms; there might have been forty or fifty. The sentry challenged, but the ruffians returned no answer, and decamped, finding us on the alert, and probably not knowing our weakness; for had we come to blows our party must have got the worst of it, though I have not the least doubt that our Affghān guard would have stood by us even against their own countrymen.

The next morning we proceeded along a very pretty road, flanked by green hedgerows full of wild flowers, and varied occasionally near the houses with parterres of roses of exquisite fragrance. My route lay to Bāber's tomb, but Capt. Westmacott being anxious to reach Cābul could not accompany me, so we parted, mutually regretting that we had so short a time to spend in this delicious region. At Bāber's tomb the Kazi of the adjacent village endeavoured to play off on me a trick, well known to old campaigners, by assuring me that unless I took from his hands a guard of at least twelve men (of course paying them for their services), my life would not be safe during the night. I refused his guard, and the only annoyance I experienced was from myriads of musquitoes, who tormented me incessantly throughout the night. I rode into camp the following day, and was delighted to find myself once more with my brother officers.

CHAPTER XIX.

On the 24th September I started on another excursion, though under very different circumstances; our party on this occasion consisting of Her Majesty's 13th Light Infantry, two companies of the 37th Native Infantry, two squadrons of the Bengal 2nd Cavalry, a small body of Affghān horsemen under Prince Timour Shah, three nine-pounders, two 24-inch howitzers, and two 8 1/2-inch mortars, the whole under the command of Sir Robert Sale, the object of the expedition being to quell some refractory chiefs inhabiting the northern and some hilly parts of the Kohistān.

It would be beyond the sphere of this little book to enter into a detailed account of our operations in the field, nor do I pretend to have sufficient materials by me for such a delicate task, in the execution of which I might by erroneous statements expose myself to just animadversion.

I had not, I regret to say, the means of ascertaining with precision the different causes which had driven these hill chiefs into rebellion. The footing which Dost Mahomed had lately acquired in the north-west encouraged them to persist, and it will be seen in the sequel, that at the disgraceful scene of Purwun Durrah the Dost was almost a *prisoner* in the hands of those who were considered, by the unversed in the intricacies of Affghān policy, to be only in arms for the restoration of their favourite to the throne of Cābul.

Were it in my power to give an accurate description of the different positions assumed by the enemy, and provided I had the leisure to survey the ground, then I am well aware that I might have claimed additional interest for my pages, as I should have elucidated the mode of warfare peculiar to the Affghāns; but such an attempt would perhaps carry me out of my depth. I must therefore be content with remarking, that though in action the Affghāns acknowledge some guiding chieftain, yet the details of position are left to each tribe. They have no confidence in each other; it follows, therefore, that the wisest plan is to turn either or both flanks, as this manoeuvre is almost sure to require a change in the original disposition of their force, which they, for want of good communications between their detached parties, are unable to effect. Hence confusion arises, and the uncertainty of support generally causes the whole to retreat. The Affghāns have great dread of their flanks being turned, and will sometimes abandon an almost impregnable position in consequence of a demonstration being made to that effect, which after all could never have been carried out.

On the third day after our departure from Cabul, the force encamped at a place called Vaugh opposite the beautiful Istālif, whose luxuriant vineyards and magnificent orchards have before excited the admiration of the traveller. But we had still some marches to get over before reaching the territories of the refractory chiefs, and it was not till the 29th that we came to Toottum Durrah, or valley of mulberries. Here we found the enemy posted in force, but it was merely an affair of detachments, two companies of the 13th and two of the 37th being ordered to make a detour to the right and left, so as to threaten the enemy's flanks. The main column closing up continued to advance; the enemy did not make a very determined resistance, yet a chance shot killed poor Edward Conolly, brother to the victim of the ruffian king of Bokhara. His--poor fellow!--was a soldier's death; though we deplore his loss, we know that he died in honorable warfare; but we have no such consolation for the fate of his poor brother, and it is with difficulty that his indignant countrymen can refrain from imprecating the vengeance of God upon the cowardly destroyer of so much talent and virtue.

The enemy made no further stand this day, and we proceeded about fifteen miles down the valley to Julghur, destroying before our departure the mud forts of Toottum Durrah. At Julghur the enemy shewed more resistance; they trusted in the strength of their fort, and we perhaps too much to its weakness. The result was, that a wing of the 13th, not more than one hundred and twenty strong, suffered a loss of fourteen men killed and seventeen wounded, and the enemy were eventually shelled out by the batteries under the direction of Capt. Abbott.

The following morning we buried our gallant companions, amongst them our respected serjeant-major (Airey), in one deep grave; but a report was current, that shortly after our departure, the bodies had been disinterred and exposed in front of the grave, that every Affghān might witness and exult in the disgrace to which they had subjected the corpses of the Feringhis.

This is but a single instance of the hatred which actuated our enemy, and when we consider the exasperating effects of these cowardly outrages on the minds of the soldiery, we should the more admire the generosity and clemency of the British in the hour of victory. I am aware that ill-informed people have accused our armies in Affghanistān, especially after the advance of General Pollock's force, of many acts of cruelty to the natives, but I can emphatically deny the justice of the accusation. Some few instances of revenge for past injuries did occur, but I am sure that an impartial soldier would rather admire the forbearance of men who for days had been marching over the mangled remains of the Cābul army.

But to return to the Kohistān. On the 4th of October we took a transverse direction westward, crossing the plain of Buggrām, supposed to be the site of the "Alexandria ad Calcem Caucasi" of the ancients; numerous coins, gems, and relics of antiquity are found hereabouts, particularly subsequently to the melting of the snows. Formerly they were considered useless, but when our enterprising countrymen and the army of the Indus found their way to Cābul, these memorials of the Greek had ready purchasers amongst the numismatologists of the British force. At the same time the Cābulese considered it great folly our exchanging the current coin for what were in their estimation useless pieces of old silver and copper.

Throughout the marches and countermarches which it was necessary for us to make in the northern districts of the Kohistān, in order to prevent the enemy from gathering together, we were much interested by the varied beauty of the scenery; and it must candidly be admitted that our ignorance as to the nature or amount of force we might any day find opposed to us by no means diminished our excitement. Rather an extraordinary phenomenon occurs in a small range of hills detached from the parent mountains, a little to the northward of the fort of Julghur. From top to bottom of the precipitous side of one of these spurs extends a light golden streak, rather thicker and less highly coloured at the bottom than at the top. I was unable to approach it nearer than about four miles, but I was credibly informed that the streak was in reality what its appearance first suggested to my mind, a body of fine sand continually flowing over the side of the hill, and depositing its volumes in a heap at the base of the mountain. I might perhaps in a windy day have ascertained the correctness of the report, as then the sandy cascade would appear as a cloud of dust, but the weather was calm during the whole time we were in its vicinity. It is called by the natives the Regrowān or flowing sand. Being no geologist, I refrain from offering any suggestions as to its cause, but merely state what I saw and heard.

After marching about the country for some days like the Paladins of old in search of adventure, we turned our faces once more towards Cābul and encamped near Kara-bagh. While here, a scene occurred which will doubtless be still in the recollection of many officers with the force, and which I relate as illustrative of the barbarous customs of the people. Many of the stories which I have introduced must of course be received by the impartial or incredulous reader "cum grano salis." I have given them as they were repeated to me, but I can personally vouch for the following fact.

Our bugles had just sounded the first call to dinner, when a few officers who were strolling in front of the camp observed a woman with a black veil walking hurriedly from some dark-looking object, and proceed in the direction of that part of the camp occupied by the Affghan force under Prince Timour Shah, the Shah Zada, heir apparent to the throne of Cābul. On approaching the object, it was discovered to be a man lying on the ground with his hands tied behind him, his throat half severed, with three stabs in his breast, and two gashes across the stomach. The mangled wretch was still breathing, and a medical man being at hand, measures were instantly taken most calculated to save his life, but without success, and in a quarter of an hour he was a corpse. Familiar as we were with scenes which in our own happy land would have excited the horror and disgust of every man possessed of the common feelings of humanity, there was something in this strange murder which caused us to make enquiries, and the reader will hardly believe me when I tell him that the victim met his fate with the knowledge and consent of Timour Shah. The woman whom we first observed was the legal murderess. She had that morning been to the Shah Zada and sworn on the Korān that the deceased many years back had murdered her husband and ran away with his other wife; she had demanded redress according to the Mahommedan law––blood for blood. The Shah Zada offered the woman a considerable sum of money if she would waive her claim to right of personally inflicting the punishment on the delinquent, and allow the man to be delivered over to his officers of justice, promising a punishment commensurate with the crime he had committed. But the woman persisted in her demand for the law of the Korān. Her victim was bound and delivered into her hands; she had him conducted in front of the prince's camp about three hundred yards off, and effected her inhuman revenge with an Affghān knife, a fit instrument for such a purpose.

Before returning to Cābul it was deemed requisite to punish the rebellious owner of the fort of Babboo-koosh-Ghur. On the approach of our force he decamped with all his vassals, and as it was advisable to leave some permanent mark of our displeasure, the bastions were blown down with gunpowder. It seems that the enemy imagined we were very negligent in camp, for they honored us the same evening with one of their night attacks, for which they are famous, the object in general being rather to harass their adversary by keeping him on the alert than to penetrate to his tents.

On the present occasion they commenced a distant fusillade upon the left of our line, extending it gradually along nearly the whole face; a few rounds of grape from the artillery soon cleared *their* front, but the enemy continued for above three hours a random fire upon the left, and, strange to say, they kept aloof from the European troops, who were encamped as usual on the right of the line. The artillery horses being picketted in soft ground soon drew their iron pegs, and having thus obtained their liberty, scampered up and down in rear of the troops and amongst the tents, thereby considerably adding to the confusion and uproar. On the alarm first sounding every light was extinguished in the camp, and well was it that these precautionary measures were adopted, for a great portion of the standing tents were riddled. The enemy fired without aim, and we were fortunate enough to lose only one sepoy; we could not ascertain the amount of casualty amongst them, but from the sudden cessation of any attack upon that part of the line where the artillery was stationed, we concluded that the rounds of grape must have told with considerable effect.

After midnight the enemy withdrew, and when at a distance of about half a mile from our outposts gave a shout of defiance, perhaps to draw a party from the camp to pursue them, which, however, was not done, or rejoicing at the havoc they imagined to have made in our ranks. We heard afterwards that the Affghāns with their usual superstition had remembered that many years ago a large army had been attacked on the same ground we then occupied and annihilated, and that probably a like success would crown their efforts in the present instance.

This night attack rendered some further demonstration of our powers of retaliation necessary, particularly as a portion of our adversaries were from the fort of Kardurrah, to which we proceeded the next day and easily captured, the enemy retiring to the hills on our advance, abandoning a strong and easily defended position, for their flank could not have been turned without incurring considerable loss, if the fort of Kardurrah had been held in a determined manner. It was generally remarked as being a particularly strong place, the approach leading through orchards surrounded by mud walls six or seven feet high and loopholed, the lanes intersecting them being barricadoed as if to be held to the last extremity.

Probably such was their valiant intention, but it seems they were bewildered by our attacking them from different points, and not trusting to each other for support, all took to their heels. The undulating ground was strewn with masses of detached rocks, and they had also built up several small but substantial stone breast-works, so that altogether we had reason to congratulate ourselves on their unexpected retreat.

The women had been previously conveyed away with the heavy baggage, and we found the houses empty, but fruit of every description was lying about the streets, prepared and packed for the winter supply of the Cābul market. Melons, peaches, pears, walnuts were either in heaps against the walls or placed in baskets for transportation; but the most curious arrangement was exhibited in the mode in which they preserved their brobdignag grapes for winter consumption. About thirty berries, each of enormous size and separately enveloped in cotton, were hermetically enclosed between a couple of rudely shaped clay saucers, so that we were obliged to crack the saucers to get at the fruit inside, and great was the scrambling amongst the thirsty soldiers for their luscious contents as they rolled out upon the ground.

CHAPTER XX.

The thread of my narrative now guides me to an event which cannot be contemplated without astonishment and regret. I allude to the unaccountable panic which seized the 2nd Cavalry during the action at Purwan Durrah; indeed I would willingly pass it over in silence, but I am anxious to express my humble admiration of the chivalrous bearing of the European officers on that melancholy occasion.

The several severe blows which we had recently inflicted upon the Affghāns during the course of this short compaign, and their not having lately appeared in any organized force in the vicinity of our camp, caused an opinion to prevail amongst many that our labours for the season were brought to a close; but on the 20th of October we were again excited by the rumour that Dost Mahommed, who had been hovering about, intended as a "dernière ressource" once more to try his fortune in war. Our anticipations of a little more active service were soon realized by an order to advance upon Purwan Durrah. We accordingly struck our tents, passing by Aukserai, and encamped near Meer Musjedi's fortress, remaining there till the 3rd of November watching the movements of the enemy. On that day information was received that the Dost, with a large body of horse and foot, was moving towards us by the Purwan Durrah; the general decided upon checking his progress, and an advanced guard consisting of four companies of the 13th under Major Kershaw, two companies of Native Infantry, two nine-pounders, and two squadrons of the 2nd Bengal Cavalry, the whole under the command of Col. Salter of the 2nd Cavalry, preceded the main column. On the road we met a follower of one of the friendly chiefs charged with a report that the ex-Ameer's party had been attacking some of the forts in the valley, but for the present had taken up a position on the neighbouring hills. We soon came on them, and at a short distance perceived a small body of cavalry in the plain. A rumour passed through our ranks that Dost Mahommed was himself amongst the horsemen, and it was a subject of congratulation that the only opportunity had now arrived of our cavalry engaging theirs, and that one brilliant attack would bring this desultory warfare to a glorious termination.

The squadrons under the command of the gallant Fraser were ordered to advance, and moved steadily forward at a trot; all eyes were fixed upon them––the men were apparently steady––and even the least sanguine could hardly doubt the result of a shock of disciplined cavalry on an irregular body of horse not half their numerical strength.

But when the word to charge was given, an uncontrolled panic seized the troopers; instead of putting their horses into a gallop and dashing forward to certain victory, the pace gradually slackened; in vain did their officers use every effort to urge the men on––in vain did the spirit-stirring trumpet sound the charge––the troopers were spell-bound by the demon of fear; the trot became a walk, then a halt; and then, forgetful of their duty, their honor, and their officers, they wheeled about and shamefully fled.

But not for one single instant did Fraser hesitate; with a bitter and well-merited expression of contempt at this unmanly desertion, he briefly said, "We must charge alone," and dashing spurs into his horse, he rushed to an almost certain fate, followed by Ponsonby, Crispin, Broadfoot, Dr. Lord, and by about a dozen of his men, who all preferred an honourable death to an ignominious life.

The feelings of disgust mingled with intense admiration with which this unparalleled scene was viewed by the infantry can be better imagined than expressed; and those who under similar trying circumstances would have endeavoured to imitate the heroism of their countrymen, could scarce subdue a thrill of horror as this handful of brave soldiers galloped forward. The intrepid Fraser, mounted upon a large and powerful English horse, literally hewed a lane for himself through the astonished Affghans; and Ponsonby too--for I am weary of seeking fresh epithets for their unsurpassable conduct--on a strong Persian mare, for a time bore down all opposition. Dost Mahommed himself, though in some personal danger from the impetuosity of this desperate charge, could not restrain his admiration.

The event fully proved the danger incurred. Dr. Lord, Crispin, and Broadfoot upheld the glory of their country to the last, and fell covered with many wounds. Fraser and Ponsonby were both desperately hacked, and owed their lives to their horses becoming unmanageable, bearing their riders from the midst of the enemy. The reins of Ponsonby's bridle were cut, and he himself grievously wounded in the face, while Fraser's arm was nearly severed in two; neither did their horses escape in the conflict, as both bore deep gashes of the Affghān blades.

While the European officers were thus sacrificing themselves in the execution of their duty, the dastard troopers came galloping in amongst the infantry of the advanced guard, some of whom were with difficulty restrained from inflicting on the spot the punishment they so well deserved.

Meanwhile the enemy's cavalry, flushed with success, advanced against the infantry with colours flying and loud shoutings, as in expectation of an easy victory. But the infantry were prepared to receive them, and a few rounds from the nine-pounders soon caused them to halt; finding that their antagonists were not under the same influence as the cavalry, they gave up the attack and retired to a distant position on the hills. The steady advance of the 37th N.I. from the main body of our forces, together with a few judiciously thrown shells, soon drove their infantry to a more elevated range of hills; and before sunset we had quiet possession of the field.

We had the melancholy satisfaction of finding the bodies of our comrades, whom we buried at night in one large grave, and performing the solemn service of the dead by torchlight. There is no chance of their being forgotten: so long as gallantry is admired and honour revered amongst British soldiers, so long will they remember Fraser's charge at Purwan Durrah.

I am loath to dwell on the misconduct of the troopers; as far as I am enabled to ascertain it was unexpected by the officers. Some, indeed, declare that previous disaffection existed amongst the men; others say that the troopers being Mussulmen did not like to charge against Dost Mahommed himself, whom they considered as their religious chief; but I think we may fairly attribute their flight to downright *cowardice*, as no complaint or cause was assigned by the men previous to encountering the foe. Whatever be the truth, the event was most unfortunate, for it appears that the Dost was even previous to the action anxious to throw himself upon the protection of the British, but his followers would not permit him to do so; nevertheless, on the evening of that day he managed to elude their vigilance, and riding directly to Cābul met the envoy Sir William M'Naghten taking his evening ride, and surrendered himself into his hands.

The news of this event of course put an end to further hostilities, and on the 7th of November we returned to Cābul, heartily glad once more to get comfortably housed, as the winter was rapidly approaching and the nights severely cold.

THE END.

LIST OF PLATES.

Frontispiece (Outer Cave at Yeermallik)

View of the Outer Cave of Yeermallik, shewing the Entrance Hole to the larger Cavern.

Map of Cabul and the Kohistan, with the Route to Koollum.

View of the Ice Caves in the Cavern of Yeermallik.

View of Koollum from the Eastward.

Fac-Simile Drawings of Ancient Coins found in Toorkisthan and Affghanistan, in the possession of Capt. Burslem, as follows:

No. 1. A Bactrian coin: legend on the obverse, [Transliterated from the Greek lettering, Basileus ermaion sot]. Reverse, Hercules on a tuckt or throne, with his right arm extended.

No. 2. A square copper coin of Apollodotus: legend, [Transliterated from the Greek lettering, Basileus pollodot soter]; a male figure, holding in one hand a club, and a spear in the other. The reverse bears Pelhvic characters.

No. 3. A square copper coin of Eucratides: [Transliterated from the Greek, Basileus megal] is only decypherable. If of Eucratides the Great, of which I have no doubt, this coin is of great value, as he reigned in Bactria 181 B.C. The reverse bears a Pelhvic legend, with the figures of two warriors mounted.

No. 4. A square silver coin of Menander. A helmeted head, with the inscription, [Transliterated from the Greek, Basileus soteros Menandrou]. The reverse bears the emblematic figure of an owl.

No. 5. A square copper coin, inscription illegible. On the obverse is a woman holding a flower or a priest offering incense. It appears to be a Kanirkos coin.

No. 6.

No.
7.

A round silver Indo-Scythian coin.

No.
8.

A square silver coin of Apollodotus, 195 B.C. Obverse, an elephant, with the Bactrian monogram beneath-- [Transliterated from the Greek, Basileus pollodoton soteros]. Reverse, an Indian bull. The characters and figures on this coin are very distinct.

No.
9.

Another coin of Menander. An elephant's head with the proboscis elevated: legend, [Transliterated from the Greek, Basileus soteros Menandrou]. On the reverse is a cannon. This is an old and valuable coin.

No.
10.

A gold coin, supposed by Lady Sale to be a Kadphises. The legend begins with Amokad and ends with Korano. On the reverse is a naked figure, with the right arm stretched out. A few specimens, but in copper, have been found in the barrow at Maunikyala in the Punjaub. Lady Sale considers this coin to be a great beauty and of value.

A gem found in the plain of Buggram.

Maps

Map of Cabul and the Kohistan, with the Route to Koollum.

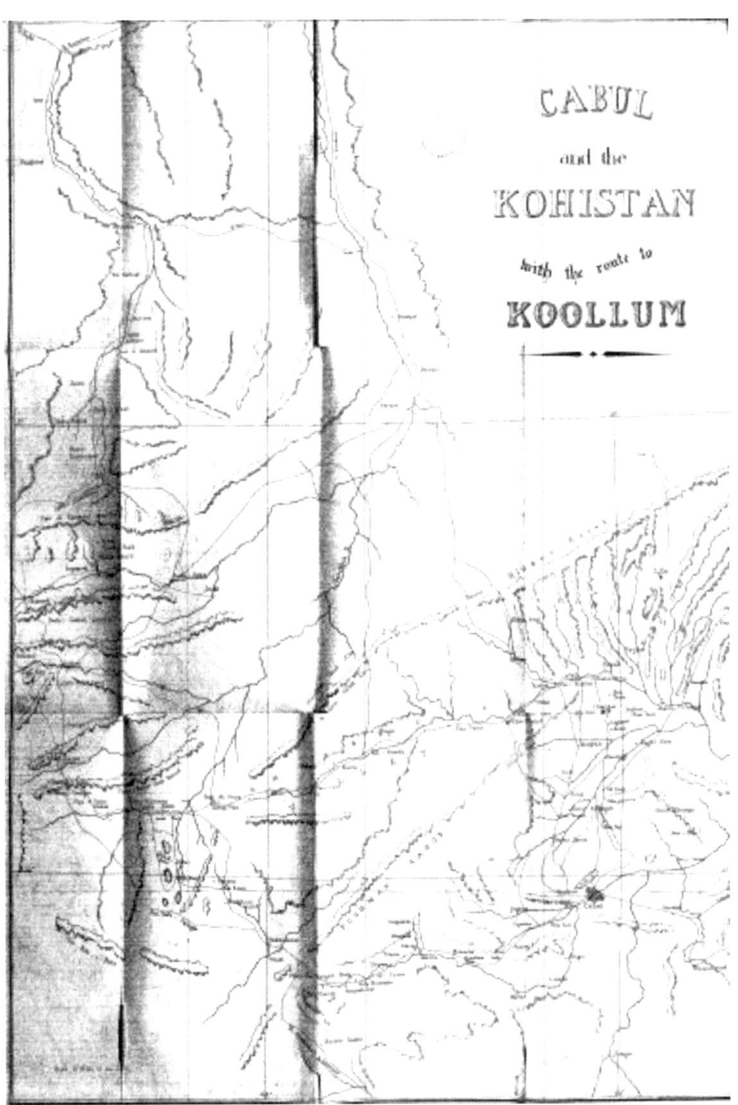

Zoom Level = 1:2, therefore Map Scale = 16 miles to an inch.